SCOTTISH FISHING VESSELS OF THE NINETEENTH CENTURY

SCOTTISH FISHING VESSELS OF THE NINETEENTH CENTURY

A Guide to Building
Scale Model Boats

Hamish Barber

Published by BookSurge, LLC – An Amazon.com company
Principal offices at 5341 Dorchester Road, Suite 16, North Charleston, SC 29418, USA.

ISBN 1-4196-2002-9

CONTENTS

PLATES

FIGURES

ACKNOWLEDGMENTS

It is with gratitude that I acknowledge the contribution that the following individuals and organizations have made to this book by giving permission for the reproduction of ship plans and photographs.

National Maritime Museum, Greenwich, London
1. Moray Firth Scaffie, *Gratitude*
2. Oban skiff, *Gylen*
3. Loch Fyne skiff, *Bonny Jean*
4. Loch Fyne skiff, *Snowdrop*
5. Largs line skiff
6. Zulu skiff, *Aye Ready*
7. Zulu skiff, *Jean Morgan*
8. Portpatrick line skiff, *Brothers*
9. Solway Firth net whammel, *Dora*

Brown, Son & Ferguson, Glasgow
1. Zulu fishing boat, *Muirneag*

The Royal National Mission to Deep Sea Fisherman
1. Fifie, *True Vine*
2. Westray Yole
3. *Bounty*, UL 217
4. Ness Yole
5. Zulu, *Fidelity* of Portessie

John Neil MacLeod
1. Plans of the Ness boat, *An Sgoth Niseach*

Executers of the Late Angus Bell
1. Plans of Moray Firth salmon cobble

Rev. Donald MacQuarrie, Fort William
1. Plans of Grimsay double ender
2. Photographs of Grimsay double ender and *An Sgoth Niseach*

The Science Museum, London
1. Plans of the Shetland Sixareen, *Water Witch*

Conway Maritime Press
1. Photographs published in *Model Shipwright*, editions 73 (page 59) and 99 (page 19)

Character Boats
1. Plans for Ullapool Post boat

Last but in no way least I wish to acknowledge the considerable help given to me by Mʳ Jim Gerbrandt, Mʳ Lindsey Thomas Martin, and Mʳ Ted Staunton (cover design) all of British Columbia, Canada, without whose help and enthusiasm it is doubtful this book would have ever seen the light of day.

FOREWORD

I have been building models since my early teenage years, mainly of boats but also of aircraft and of fighting vehicles from the second World War. All the models were built from kits, and these were mainly plastic, although I remember building several galleons from balsa wood before plastic became readily available.

In the late Autumn of 1971 I bought a Billing boat kit of a Danish crabber, which looked for all the world exactly like a traditional Scottish motorised fishing boat of the 1960s. This for me was a boat kit with a difference: it was a wood kit, with all necessary pieces accurately machined so that a clinker-built or clench-built boat emerged from the amazing assortment of pieces of wood. Not only was the boat clench built but the method of building seemed to me to be as close to the way a full-sized boat would have been built as was possible.

I planned to build more Billing boats but I found myself unable to relate to what seemed to me to be a collection of a variety of foreign boats of many different types and with each kit at a different scale. Then, in 1974 I visited the excellent museum in Lerwick, which houses a variety of models of old Scottish, and particularly Shetland, boats. The only disappointments were that, once again, no two boats were at the same scale so that comparisons were difficult to make and there did not seem to be any West Coast boats in the collection. I was particularly impressed with a magnificent model of a Zulu fishing boat, and almost there and then decided that I would build a collection of Scottish fishing boats of the nineteenth and early twentieth centuries; and build them all to the same scale. This last decision seemed to me to be important so that accurate comparisons of size and weight of construction could be made among different craft, reflecting the different sea conditions in which each would operate.

I had no idea where I could find plans of fishing boats of the nineteenth century. Some months later I came across an article on 'Woods to use in model boat building' in the magazine, *Model Boats*, and written by Ewart Freeson. I wrote to him, asking not only about sources of the different types of wood that he had described but also if he knew where I could find plans of old Scottish fishing boats. His reply introduced me to the collection of plans prepared by Philip Oke in the 1930s under the auspices of the Society for Maritime Research.

Philip Oke was a Merchant Navy officer and spent most of his available spare time drawing plans of as many existing sail or oar-driven commercial craft as could be found round the shores of Britain. He never finished his task as the second World War, in which he was lost, began before he had finished. Ewart Freeson's other bit of news was that all the Oke plans were housed in the National Maritime Museum in Greenwich and that photocopies, to any scale, could be purchased from the Museum by post.

Although I had the experience of building the clench-hulled crabber from Billing, I had no knowledge or understanding of the techniques of building clench and carvel hulls. I obtained copies of the two-part book by Harold Underwood, *Plank-on-Frame Models*, published by Brown, Son & Ferguson in 1958 but now sadly out of print. In the first volume Underhill describes, step by step, the construction of the brigantine 'Leon' all the way to the spars, rigging and metal work required. The second volume has a chapter entitled 'Clinker-built models' and, with both of these references, I was able to make a hesitant start to my goal of building a collection of models of nineteenth-century Scottish fishing boats. My only criticism of these books, and of more recent such publications, is that the boats that are described tend to be complex and of some considerable difficulty, and I felt the need for a book that sets out clearly the technique of building an open clench-built hull and a carvel hull, with the ways of completing the interiors and spars, of what are really quite basic craft.

This book sets out to do just that, giving detailed step-by-step descriptions of building an open, clench-built, 1850 Fifie and a decked carvel Fifie of about 1880. Additionally I have included the plans of more than 20 Scottish nineteenth-century fishing vessels, all taken from the original craft during the first half of the twentieth century. It is my hope that this book will be of help to those who wish to take up this fascinating hobby but who, like me, do not know where and how to begin. From natural and personal preference I have concentrated solely on Scottish fishing boats of the nineteenth and early twentieth centuries but the construction methods described below can be applied to virtually any sail-driven, small commercial craft of these years.

Hamish Barber

SCOTTISH FISHING VESSELS OF THE NINETEENTH CENTURY

CHAPTER I: A BRIEF HISTORY OF COMMERCIAL FISHING IN SCOTLAND

The earliest known settlement in Britain dates back over 30,000 years, when visits by hunter-gatherers from what is now Europe, to which the island later known as Britain was joined, were occasional and sporadic. The last ice age was at its most intense 18,000 years ago, although there was a lesser return to these conditions about 11,000 years ago, and the weather returned to a warmer and more benevolent climate about 8,500 years ago. From that date onwards Scotland became a more welcoming territory for year-long human habitation.

The earliest established site of human occupation in Scotland is on the island of Rum in the inner Hebrides where, 9,000 years ago, a group of hunter-gatherers created a settlement. These settlers must have come from the south and were probably initially seasonal visitors but, since Rum is an island, they must have arrived by sea. Excavated middens on Rum and many other sites in western Scotland contain fish bones that are evidence that deep-sea fishing was practised, probably from sea-going, skin-covered coracles, which would also have been the means by which the earliest peoples both reached islands such as Rum and were able to trade blood-stone tools, made from a rock found only in Rum, with groups of hunter-gatherers on other islands and on the mainland. So, sea-going coracles were probably in common use as far back as 9,000 years ago and evidence of deep-sea fishing – the excavated remains of fish that normally inhabit deep water – has been found in the middens around settlements. Thus, a tradition of gaining food from the sea – fishing – had become established.

Fishing probably existed as a 'cottage industry', meeting only the immediate needs of a family or village, until the eighteenth century, although earlier Scottish Kings had promulgated laws on the sale and the export of fish, laws that mainly affected the east-coast ports of Fife, Angus and Aberdeen. During the seventeenth and eighteenth centuries the herring fishing in the North Sea was dominated by the Dutch who not only had immense fleets of 'Herring Busses' but had a monopoly on methods of curing the catch. The fleets of Busses, some 4,000 strong, were regularly guarded by ships of the Dutch

Navy and followed the herring shoals in the North Sea from the north of Scotland to the south-east coast of England.

Dutch cured herrings were a luxury commodity attracting high prices in Europe and the Dutch jealously protected this monopoly. During the early 1700s bounties were offered by the British Government to encourage Scottish fishermen to capture more of the herring trade but the size and construction of boats at that period were severely limited by the absence of harbours, the need to be able to drag boats up a beach to a position above high tide, the limitations on the length of strakes that could be obtained in one piece from a tree to plank a boat and the availability of finance.

In 1786 the British Fisheries Society was established by an Act of Parliament, funded largely by ex-patriot and wealthy Scots business men in London with some moneys being allocated from estates sequestered after the 1745 Rising. The remit of the Society was to encourage the development of fishing – mainly herring fishing – in Scotland. While herring shoals of immense proportions were common and annual visitors to both the west Highland sea-lochs and along the east coast of Britain from Wick to Lowestoft, a number of practical difficulties existed in the exploitation of this resource. Boats were generally small and could not venture far out to sea and certainly for not more than one or two days. It was usual for boats to set sail for the fishing grounds in the early evening, lie to their nets overnight and return to their home ports in the morning. Harbours were mainly non-existent or primitive in their facilities, transport by road of salt for curing herring, barrels in which to pack cured herring and the means to enable the catch, suitably cured and barrelled, to reach southern markets were difficult or non-existant and, thus, a number of factors acted together to prevent the further development of what was a huge and important potential harvest.

In 1788 the British Fisheries Society established a fishing settlement at Loch Broom but for various reasons this venture was a failure and the station was abandoned in 1791. Between 1788 and 1790 a larger settlement was built at Ullapool, which after initial difficulties and problems ultimately thrived, and at about the same time plans were developed to establish a fishing settlement at Tobermory. This failed as a fishing port but became successful in handling general cargoes for the inner and outer Hebrides.

By 1790 the number of fishing boats on the north-east coast had increased so dramatically that there seemed to be an urgent need for a safe harbour in that region. Between 1803 and 1830 the harbour and fishing station at Pultneytown, Wick, was built by the Society and this proved to be the main base for the immense fishing fleets that annually followed the shoals of herring southwards down the east coasts of Scotland and England during the latter half of the nineteenth century. By the late 1800s there were three herring fishing seasons – the winter season from January to March, mainly out of Wick and Stornoway, the early herring season in May and June and the summer season which involved boats following the shoals of herring southwards to Essex, from July to the end of the year.

The absence of safe harbours and the fact that the great majority of boats were both small and open resulted in the frequent and repeated loss of fishing boats and crews when unexpected gales occurred. For example, in 1839 20 boats lying in the harbour at Scartlet were destroyed by a sudden gale and in 1845 30 boats were destroyed at Forse, while many more were lost at sea.

An August gale in 1848 brought this incessant problem to the notice of the Government. In a short period of little more than 24 hours a total of 124 boats were sunk or damaged on the north-east coast and over 100 fishermen were lost at sea. A Government inquiry was conducted, which resulted in the *Washington Report* being published in October 1849 and a number of problems being identified. Harbours were few and far between, often not well maintained, with entrances blocked by discarded boulders and other debris, missing lights on piers so that at night a cottage lamp could be mistaken for the pier-head light; and the fishing boats in general use were small and open and without decks. After a successful night's fishing the boat could be so loaded that the freeboard was less than twelve inches, so that a sudden wave could swamp and sink the boat within minutes.

Improvements were slow in coming. Over the next 30 years the number and state of harbours were improved and with this came the further development of larger and decked boats. The *Washington Report* included the plans of six north-east coast boats, all of which were open, clench-built craft, none much larger that 35 feet. Fully decked boats were enthusiastically promoted but were largely rejected by the fishing community because of the attendant dangers when working in rough weather on a deck set only a foot below the gunwale. By the latter part of the nineteenth century, however, most east-coast boats could lie afloat alongside a harbour wall, boats had become steadily larger, thus able to hold a greater catch, and fully decked craft had become accepted by the fishing community. From 1870 until the development of steam-driven fishing boats in the early 1900's the herring fleets, sometimes as many as 2,000 strong, consisted mainly of Zulus and Fifies with keel lengths of more than 70 feet. The advent of steam power in the latter years of the nineteenth century, soon to be followed by petrol-paraffin engines and ultimately by diesel power spelt the death of sail-driven fishing boats and the concept of drift netting as opposed to trawling as a means of catching fish.

CHAPTER 2: DESIGN OF FISHING BOATS THROUGH THE CENTURIES

Wooden fishing boats of the nineteenth century were basically of two methods of construction: clench, or clinker, and carvel built. Prior to the development of harbours where boats could lie afloat against a pier wall, the preferred method of construction was clench built. This involved overlapping planks, or strakes, of wood which resulted in the strength of the hull being obtained by the overlap of strakes, the 'lands' where one strake rested on the one below. The ribs, or frames, were light and did no more than 'stress' the strong hull. The hull was further strengthened by longitudinal lengths of wood from stern to stem, stringers, that supported the lower deck and the thwarts. The result was a boat that was light for her size, immensely strong for her weight and able to bend and move with the motion of the sea. This was a method of construction that was particularly important where there was no sheltered harbour and when the boat had to be dragged up the beach to above the high water mark at the end of each night's fishing. The clench method of construction had been perfected by the Vikings in the ninth century and was to persist until the latter half of the nineteenth century.

The disadvantage of clench building was that the hull strakes had to be continuous, and the length of the boat was thus governed by the length of a plank of wood that could be cut from a tree trunk. The largest clench built boats were thus seldom more than 34 feet, with a corresponding reduction in their load carrying capacity. All the pre-1850 boats were also open boats with the deck some three or three and a half feet below the gunwale. While this gave a measure of safety to the men working on board, especially in rough seas, it also meant that a good catch of herring might see the boat with little more than a foot's freeboard so that a sudden squall or an unexpected wave could swamp the boat, with dire results.

With the increase along the North Sea coast in the number of harbours, where fishing boats could lie alongside a pier or harbour wall, carvel construction became the method of choice. Once the keel has been laid and erected in a building frame, a number of strong ribs, or frames, are then constructed and fitted to the keel. The frames are usually about two feet apart so that in a seventy foot boat there are 35 or so frames. The planks are then fastened to the frames, butting against one another with no overlap, and thus one length of strake can consist of several lengths of wooden plank. In contrast to clench building where the strength of the hull rests with the overlapping strakes, the strength of the carvel built hull is in the massive ribs or frames. A carvel built boat of seventy feet keel length, as were the big Zulus and Fifies in the latter two decades of the nineteenth century, cannot be hauled up a beach and had to remain afloat against the harbour wall, but this method of construction did allow boats of considerably greater size to be built, with the corresponding increase in profitability. The big Zulus and Fifies that dominated the last two decades of the nineteenth century had keel lengths in excess of 70 feet, could carry an immense catch of herring and could sail at upwards of 16 knots with a good wind.

Sadly, by the 1910s steam power had ousted sail-driven fishing boats and in a relatively short period of time steam had given way to diesel power and all too inevitably to the modern boats with their immense catching power. Some, originally sail-driven, boats were converted to power but this was a compromise and lasted only a few years. In Loch Dochfour, just north of where Loch Ness links with the Caledonian Canal near Inverness are the decaying hulls of two large Fifies, perhaps left there to rot in the 1920s when the combination of the depression and the dominance of powered fishing boats finally spelled the end of sail (Plate 1).

Plate 1. Decaying fishing boats in Loch Dochfour, Inverness.

The most popular and successful Moray Firth boat of the nineteenth century was the Scaffie, characterised by a rounded fore-foot and a steeply angled stern post. Early boats were open decked and of the order of 20 feet in length but, by the middle of the century, their length had increased to 30 feet or so. The boats were clench built but following the *Washington Report* of 1849 it became usual for a deck to be added above the thwarts, giving the boats a very distinctive appearance. The Scaffie was a good sea boat when working into a wind but her short keel made her a difficult boat to handle down wind.

Two other designs were also common and in the latter years of the nineteenth century tended to dominate the North Sea fisheries. The Fifie was characterised by having a vertical sternpost and an equally vertical stem, and originated, as the name suggests, in the Firth of Forth. While the Fifie was somewhat slow in tacking into the wind, the long keel meant that the boat's performance downwind was very impressive. Fifies, again, started as boats of 30 feet long but by the end of the century keels of 70 feet were common.

Tradition dates the evolution of the Zulu type boat to the imminent wedding between a Moray coast fisherman and the daughter of another seaman. The groom decided to have a new boat built and set his mind on a Fifie while his prospective father-in-law favoured a Scaffie. A compromise was reached with the new boat having the vertical stemhead of the Fifie and the steeply angled sternpost of the Scaffie. The boat was built, and called the *Nonesuch*, but the design of the boat became so popular that the class name was changed by common usage to the Zulu, in recognition of the Zulu wars in South Africa, which were at the time dominating public interest. The Zulu combined the advantages of the Scaffie with those of the Fifie, being a good sea boat both into the wind and down wind, and eventually became the dominant herring drifter until she fell an inevitable victim to the relentless advance of engine power.

CHAPTER 3: EXISTING PLANS OF OLD FISHING BOATS

Mention has been made of the plans of sail and oar working boats drawn by Philip Oke during the 1930s and of the plans of pre-1849 boats included in the *Washington Report* of 1849. The plans in the *Washington Report* are of a Wick fishing boat of about 28 feet overall length, a Peterhead boat of about 32 feet keel length, a Fraserburgh boat of 36 feet overall length, an Aberdeen boat, a Buckie boat of 41 feet and a Newhaven Fifie of 34 feet overall length. These were open boats with a deck 3 or 3 ½ feet below the gunwale amidships and with the greatest beam about one third of the length of the boat from the stern. All were clench built as this was the usual method of construction and this method of building persisted until the construction of deep-water harbours allowed the development of large carvel-built boats in the latter third of the nineteenth century.

The early plans in the *Washington Report* are limited in the information that they give: they comprise a sheer plan, with the boat viewed from the side, a body plan and a half-breadth plan, as if the boat were seen from above. By contrast, Philip Oke's plans are much more complete: in addition to a sheer plan, a full-breadth plan and occasionally a sail plan, the hull plans include a wealth of detail as to the internal fittings of the boat. The deck, thwarts, mast steps or trunks, the gear for standing rigging and many other fittings are all detailed so that a very accurate replica of the original boat can be built.

The equally detailed plans, on three sheets, of a large Zulu, *Muirneag*, were taken off the boat in 1946 before she was broken up, incredibly for wood for fence posts, and drawn by Harold Underhill who also published in 1960 a two-part book titled *Plank-on-Frame Models*. The detail in these plans is surprising but as I have yet not built this boat I cannot comment on whether the detail helps or complicates the construction.

Some years ago I read a newspaper account of how the owner of the firm, Character Boats, based in Leicester, had discovered the remains of a small lug-sailed boat that had been used between 1905 and 1920 by a postman in Ullapool to ferry the mails across Loch Broom. After making contact with the owner, he kindly supplied me with photographs of the boat together with a rough sheer plan. This was a 12-foot, open, transom-sterned, clench-built boat fitted with a single lug sail and, although no replica of this boat is in Ullapool Museum, I have made three such boats at 1:12 scale. Incredibly, although each boat has been built from the same set of plans, each has turned out subtly different; but then that is how things would have been in real life at the start of the twentieth century.

In Lewis, and particularly in the fishing village of Ness, the An Sgoth Niseach, an open boat of about 32 feet overall length, clench built on frames, was commonly used for cod and ling fishing in the often wild seas of the Atlantic at the close of the nineteenth century. A full-sized replica was built in Stornoway in 1994 and fortunately I have a set of plans of this boat, although I have yet to build a model of her.

The most exciting search for plans started in about 1989 when I read a letter to the editor in the magazine, *Yachting World*. The writer asked for any information about a 1911 Shetland boat called the *Veng*, which her family had owned for some years during the 1970s. I wrote to the writer, who lived in Plockton, telling her of my interest in building replicas of old boats and asked if by chance she had any plans of the *Veng*. Some days later I received from her a set of plans taken off the boat when she was converted from a working boat to a pleasure yacht in 1936. The letter also told me who had made the conversion – a Mr. Moncreiff of Lerwick – and despite the passage of time I chanced my arm and wrote to him. To my great surprise and pleasure, Mr. Moncreiff replied, giving me the history of the boat, her original names and a rather faded photocopy of a photograph taken of the boat on her launch date in 1911.

The importance of the *Veng*, or *Owners Delight* to give her her original name, was that, although she had the traditional lines of a Viking Shetland boat of 1911, she was the first Shetland boat to be fitted with an engine. The original engine was a Bolsover steam engine but this proved to be inefficient and after a change to an Alpha hot-bulb engine, a 30-horse-power Kelvin was installed. At her launch she was still fitted with a foresail, a gaff and a mizzen sail in addition to her steam engine.

I thus had a set of plans of the hull of the boat after her conversion to a sailing yacht and I knew that no change would have been made to the basic construction or shape of the hull. In addition, I had a rather faded photocopy of the deck lay-out of the boat at her launch in 1911 and, with a bit of hope and realism and after a prototype had been built, a reasonable 1:12 model of this boat was made, and is now in the Scottish Fisheries Museum in Anstruther.

The following table indicates all the sets of boat plans in my possession and the source of the plans.

Plans in author's possession	Figure	Source
Buckie, Wick, Fraserburgh, Peterhead, Newhaven and Aberdeen boats	5–10	Washington Report, 1849
Scaffie yawl, *Gratitude*, BCK 252, L.O.A. – 26 ft., built 1896 at Portnockie (Oke)	11–13	Philip J. Oke, National Maritime Museum, London
Fifie, *True Vine*, ML 20, L.O.A. – 71 ft., c. 1905	14–16	Edgar March, Chatham Publishing
Zulu, *Fidelity* of Portessie	17–19	Philip J. Oke, Edgar March, Chatham Publishing
Zulu, *Muirneag*	20–24	Harold A. Underhill

Plans in author's possession	Figure	Source
Moray Firth coble	25–29	Angus Bell
Westray yole, *Am Bo Torraich*	30–32	Edgar March, Chatham Publishing
Shetland engined haddock boat, *Owner's Delight*	35, 36	Gavin McLaren
Shetland sixareen, *Water Witch*	37	Lawrence Dunn, Science Museum, London
Shetland foureen	38	The Author
Ness boat, *An Sgoth Niseach*	39–41	John Neil MacLeod
Ness yole	42	Edgar March, Chatham Publishing
Grimsay double-ender, *Welcome Home*	43, 44	Rev. D. MacQuarrie
Fifie skiff, *Bounty*, UL 217, L.O.A. – 23 ft., c. 1880	45	Edgar March, Chatham Publishing
Duncan the Post's Boat, Ullapool	46	Bill Bailiff, Character Boats
Oban skiff, *Gylen*	47, 48	National Maritime Museum, London
Half-decked Zulu, *Bonnie Jean*	49	National Maritime Museum, London
Zulu skiff, *Snowdrop* of Ardrishaig	50, 51	National Maritime Museum, London
Largs line skiff	52, 53	National Maritime Museum, London
Zulu skiff, *Aye Ready*	54	National Maritime Museum, London
Zulu skiff, *Jean Morgan*	55	National Maritime Museum, London
Portpatrick line skiff, *Brothers*	56, 57	National Maritime Museum, London
Solway Firth net whammel, *Dora*	58, 59	National Maritime Museum, London

CHAPTER 4: BUILDING A CLENCH-BUILT OPEN BOAT

The plans

The *Washington Report* included outline plans of six fishing boats that were in common usage in 1845 and I have used a Newhaven Fifie as the subject of the following description of the method of constructing such a boat. The Fifie, which I have named *Silver Harvest*, is an open, clench-built boat, 34 feet from stem to stern post, carrying two masts each of 30 feet, two dipping lug sails and four 18-foot long oars. The plans of the boat, which are rather rudimentary, comprise a sheer plan, a half-breadth plan and a body plan and are shown in Plates 2 & 3.

The sheer plan shows the outline of the boat when viewed from one side and has ten vertical lines, called station lines, drawn vertically along the length of the hull. These are continuous with the lines on the half-breadth plan immediately below the sheer plan. The body plan (Plate 3) shows the curve of the hull when viewed from either bow or stern, and the sections marked 1 to 4 and A to D correspond to similar notations on the sheer plan. In practical terms a number of station lines will be selected to form the shape of the temporary building frames that are later set up on the building board. The selection of station lines for forming the building frames is a matter of personal choice: the importance of the building frames is to ensure that the curve of the planks, or strakes, corresponds to the curve of the gunwale and hull as seen on the half-breadth plan. Before starting any work it is important to draw on the sheer plan a continuation of the stem and stern posts upwards for one inch, draw a line from the top of the stem to the stern posts and continue the selected station lines up to that horizontal line (Plate 2).

Plate 2. Newhaven Fifie,1848 (sheer and half-breadth plans).

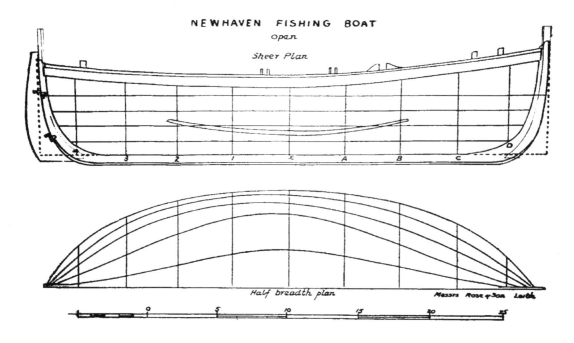

Plate 3. Newhaven Fifie, 1848 (body plan).

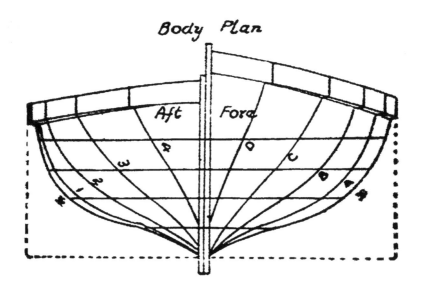

What wood?

For model boat building it is important to use wood that has little or no grain and no knots. The best woods for the construction of keel, strakes, thwarts and all other parts of the basic hull are lime or American basswood (often called American Limewood). Both of these woods can be carved and cut to very fine tolerances and give a very smooth finish for varnishing or painting. Lime wood can be obtained in sheet form, three feet by four inches, while basswood comes in lengths of two feet. Both woods can be obtained in sheets of $^1/_{32}$, $^1/_{16}$, ⅛, ¼ and ½ inch thicknesses from maritime model shops.

Other woods have their place in the construction of model boats and I have used mahogany, walnut, sycamore and pear to add a touch of contrasting colours and graining to internal fittings or deck thwarts. All of these woods, and many more, are obtainable from specialist hobby shops.

What tools are required?

Tools can be subdivided into essential and luxury items and the descriptions given below represent my personal choice. Essential tools include a craft knife, a flexible ruler, a miniature drill, a miniature set square, a vibrating saw, a miniature circular saw, clothes pegs (more of that later) and needle and larger files. The other tools that I use include a band saw, a miniature circular sander, proportional dividers and clamps of various sizes.

Vibrating **and circular saws** *(Plate 4)* The vibrating saw has a very slender fretsaw blade and vibrates, as the name suggests, rather than moving vertically. This saw is ideal for cutting complex shapes in wood of up to ¼ inch thickness. The circular saw has a fine and a course blade and is essential for cutting deck planks and other straight line pieces in wood up to ¼ inch thick.

Bandsaw (Plate 5) This is a much heavier saw and is used to cut straight or slightly curved lines in wood up to one inch in thickness.

Miniature wood drill (Plate 6) The drill accepts drill pieces from one to five millimetres in diameter and is an essential tool, used either in the drill stand or in the hand when drilling the countless holes for bamboo dowels.

Orbital sander (Plate 7) This is useful in the rough sanding of a piece, which then needs to be completed by hand.

The glue that seems best is fast-acting wood adhesive, which sets within a short period of time and is stronger than the wood itself. All parts of my models are additionally fastened with wooden trenails made from garden cane. Pieces of cane, cut from between the knuckles of the bamboo, are divided longitudinally into about eight lengths with the craft knife and trimmed until each piece is about $^1/_{16}$ inch in diameter. The pieces are then progressively pulled through the decreasing holes in a professional draw-plate until they are both round and approximate to the size of the drill used to cut

Plate 4. Vibrating and circular saws.

Plate 5. Bandsaw.

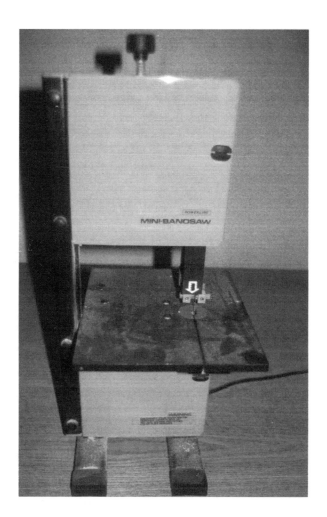

Plate 6. Miniature wood drill.

Plate 7. Orbital sander.

the holes for each dowel. A draw plate, which can be purchased from a supplier to the jewelery trade, has a succession of holes of decreasing diameters, one side of each hole being countersunk while the other is flush with the steel plate. The length of bamboo dowel is fed in to the flush side and 'drawn' through the hole, which strips off wood from the sides of the dowel (Plate 8). Generally, the dowels that I use are either $^1/_{16}$ or $^1/_{32}$ inch in diameter and the combination of glue and dowelling of each part makes the construction exceedingly strong and permanent.

The building board

A board of wood, longer and wider than the finished hull, is marked with a pencil-drawn centre line, with the position of the selected station lines drawn at right angles. For the construction of this boat I have selected station lines 1, 3, A and C as being sufficient to produce the required curve of the hull and gunwale. Clench-built boats were frequently built upside down, as this model will be, and it is important to make the temporary building frames and the stem and sternpost at least 1 inch longer than they have to be so that there is enough room for fingers to attach the final, gunwale, strake. This is the reason why extensions were drawn on the plans to the stem and stern posts and the station lines.

The four temporary building frames, 1, 3, A and C are drawn on tracing paper from the body plan; make sure that the top part of each is carried up to the pencil line already drawn on the sheer plan. The outline of the frame is then marked on ⅛ inch plywood with carbon paper and the frame is then cut out. A slot is cut into the apex of the frame into which the keel will sit. A clear pencil line is drawn across the widest part of each frame marking the level of the gunwale at each frame. As the keel will be ¼ inch in width and will project a similar distance into the frame, the cut is therefore ¼ by ¼ inch. The frames are held in position by small blocks of wood screwed into the building board (Plate 10) while the extended ends of the stem and stern posts are secured by screws to the base of the building board.

Building the keel

The shape and dimensions of the keel assembly are drawn from the sheer plan onto ¼-inch wood using tracing and carbon paper. The keel assembly comprises five parts (Plate 9): the keel, the stem and stern posts, and the deadwoods that strengthen the acute angles between the stem and stern and the keel itself. It is important that the stem and stern posts be separate from the keel so that the grain of the wood lies on the long axis of the stem and sternpost for strength. The five component parts of the keel assembly are then glued and dowelled, after which a rabbet is cut along both sides of the keel to receive one edge of the first strake to be attached, and up the stern and stem posts to receive the ends of each strake. The line of the rabbet is marked on the keel assembly in pencil, ½ inch up from the bottom of the keel and the same distance, if possible, from the front of the stem post and the back of the stern post. The rabbet is then cut using

Plate 8. Draw plate, lengths of bamboo and finished dowels.

Plate 9. The keel assembly.

Plate 10. The keel assembly in the building jig.

the point of the craft knife, creating a 'v'-shaped groove slightly wider at the open end than the thickness of the strakes and about ¹/₁₆ inch in depth. In this boat the strakes will be ¹/₁₆ inch in thickness.

The next task is to mark the positions where the topmost side of each strake will cross the frames and the stern and the stem posts. Since the boat is widest amidships and narrowest at bow and stern, the shape of each strake will be narrower towards the bow and stern and widest where the boat's width is greatest. Place a narrow slip of paper – writing paper is appropriate – with one end in the rabbet and the long axis of the paper along the edge of the building frame and mark on the paper where the top of the gunwale lies. This boat will have ten strakes on each side and the distance from one end of the piece of paper to where the gunwale line has been drawn now needs to be divided into ten equal sections on each of the frames. This can be done using a ruler but is much more easily accomplished with proportional dividers. The position of the top of each of the ten strakes is then marked on the edge of the frame, and the process is repeated for each frame and for the stem and stern posts (Plate 11).

Fitting the garboard strakes

As the boat is being built upside down, the first strake to be fitted is the garboard strake, the strake adjoining the keel. In the description of strake fitting that follows the term 'upper edge' applies to the upper edge of the strake when the hull is in the building frame.

Cut a length of planking, in this case from a sheet of lime wood 4 inches by 36 inches, at least half as wide again as the distance from the rabbet to the widest plank mark on the frames. The edge that will fit into the rabbet may require to be sanded down and will need to be cut in a slightly concave manner so that it lies comfortably against the

Plate 11. Frames with positions of strakes marked.

side of the keel. When this is done, mark the positions of the frames, the stem and the stern posts on the strake and mark also the width of the strake at each of these points. This is where the marks already pencilled on the frames and stern and stem post become essential. Using a flexible ruler draw a pencil line joining all the marks from stem to stern and cut out the strake using the craft knife. Finally, check that the cut-out strake accurately fits the rabbet in the keel and lies along the series of marks that have been made on the stem and stern post and the frames. If necessary – and this in my experience is a frequent occurrence – repeat the whole procedure until an accurate fit is obtained without having to stress the wood in any way.

The edges where one plank meets the next at the stem and stern posts of a clench-built boat are tapered so that there is a final inch or so at the bow and stern where the planks thus run into each other without an apparent overlap. This means that the lower edge of the first, or garboard, plank for about an inch at the bow and stern at this scale, needs to be pared with the craft knife so that will it run smoothly into the next strake when that strake is fitted. Before fitting the first strake – and this applies to every strake on the boat – draw the outline of the final shape of the strake on the sheet of lime wood to act as the basis for the corresponding strake on the other side of the boat. When it is certain that the strake fits cleanly onto the keel assembly, and has been sanded down, glue the edges of the strake where they meet the rabbet on the keel and the stem and stern posts and hold the strake in position with clips (Plate 12).

Once the glue has set, drill and dowel the plank into the keel, the stem and the stern posts at intervals of one inch, using dowels of $1/16$ inch diameter, pressing the dowel into the wood with the head of a clothes peg. If undue force is required, the dowel is too thick.

Plate 12. The garboard strake in position and being glued.

Fitting the remaining strakes

There now remain a further nine strakes to be fitted on each side. The procedure for shaping and fitting the strakes is essentially the same as for the garboard strake, except that both the upper and lower sides of strakes two to nine need to be pared for an inch or so from where they meet the stem and stern post so that the strakes flow into each other at these points.

Once the lower edges of the garboard and all subsequent strakes have been cut and fitted to the keel, draw a pencil line about ⅛ inch along the lower edge of the strake. This represents the 'lands' and thus where there is an overlap of the next strake on the one already in position. The width of the new strake is thus from the pencil mark, not the lower edge of the strake, to the next pencil mark on the frame. The new strake is again drawn out on the plank of lime wood, to act as the outline of the corresponding strake on the other side of the boat, and again the strake is glued along its length at the narrow 'lands' and where it meets the stem and stern post, and held, most conveniently by clothes pegs and a bulldog clip, at either end (Plate 13).

Continue to fit the strakes as has been described until strake number nine has been fitted. The only difference with the final strake is that while the upper edge at the bow and stern will be pared to flow into the previous strake, the final, tenth, strake is not pared at it's lower end. The benefit of having left the stem and stern posts, and the building frames, at least one inch longer than they need to be is now realised since it is possible for the thickest fingers to manipulate this final strake into position (Plates 14 and 15).

Plate 13. The second strake being held and glued.

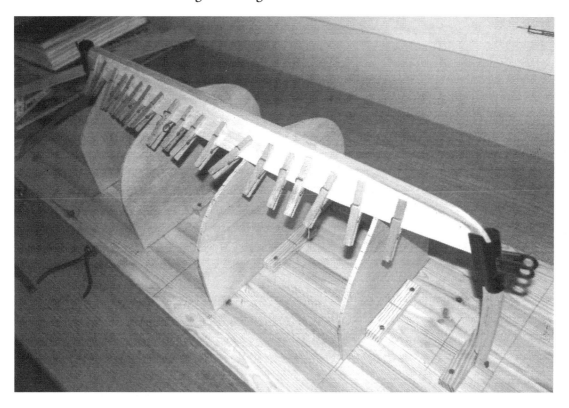

Plate 14. Planked hull from outside.

Plate 15. Inside view of hull.

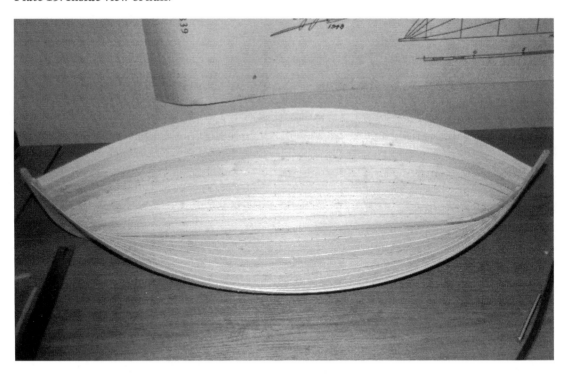

Fitting the breasthooks and the wales

The screws holding the stem and stern post to the building frame can now be removed, the hull lifted out of the building frame, and the extra one inch or so that had been added to the stem and stern posts can be cut off. While the hull will feel both light and extremely strong for it's weight, additional strength needs to be added: breasthooks at bow and stern and either an in-wale or out-wale or, as in the case of *Silver Harvest*, both. The breasthooks are shown at bow and stern in Plates 16 and 17 and are cut to shape from ¼ inch lime or bass wood. These are, as ever, glued and dowelled through the topmost plank and greatly increase the strength of the hull at stem and stern.

The out-wale is a piece of sanded wood ⅛-inch square, trimmed to fit accurately to the angles of the stem and stern post, glued and dowelled in position and held with clothes pegs until the glue has dried. *Silver Harvest* is 34 inches long and thus both the dimensions and the length of the pieces of wood used for the wales are greater than if the boat was smaller or of a different scale, and fitting the out-wale thus is more difficult. The method used is to make sure that the cut of the length and of both ends of the out-wale will give a good fit at the stem and stern posts. Then the out-wale is glued and dowelled at the stern and along about three inches of the upper edge of the topmost strake, holding the out-wale in position with clothes pegs until the glue has set and the dowels have been inserted. A thin strip of glue is then applied to the upper edge of the topmost strake, the out-wale is curved round the strake, held in position by clothes pegs and clamps, and the final inch or so, where the out-wale meets the stemhead, is then glued and dowelled. For this you really need three hands, or the help of another person.

Plate 16. Bow breasthook.

Plate 17. Stern breasthook

Once the out-wale has been fastened securely at bow and stern the intervening length is dowelled at intervals of one inch and then sanded smooth. The procedure is then repeated on the other side (Plate 18).

Most clench built boats had either an out- or an in-wale but *Silver Harvest* has both, so after the out-wales are fitted, exactly similar in-wales are fastened between the squared off ends of the bow and stern breasthooks. The hull is now extremely strong, and the combination of glue and bamboo dowels ensures that none of the parts already fitted will come apart.

Fitting the timbers or 'ribs'

The hull strength of a clinker or clench built boat lies in the continuous length of the strakes, from bow to stern, and the overlap between the upper and lower edge of each of the strakes, the 'lands', and so the timbers or ribs are relatively light in weight and in dimension and are fitted after the hull has been completed.

Strips of ⅛ by ¹/₁₆ inch lime wood are used for the timbers. Lime wood is sufficiently flexible to be stressed between the inside of the keel and the underside of the in-wale, thus ensuring a close fit against the inside of the hull. Each timber is then secured along its length with dowels through each strake (Plate 19). The timbers are fitted at intervals of one inch starting at the mid point of the keel and extending to the stern and the stem post. At the bow two additional pieces of wood, ¼ inch square, are fitted to the third and fourth timbers, and to the third timber at the stern, to form heavier timbers that project one inch above the level of the gunwale. The purpose of these extensions will be commented upon later.

Fitting the stringers, mast steps and deck beams

Once all the timbers have been fitted, glued and dowelled, two lengths of ¼ inch square wood need to be fitted on each side along the length of the inside of the hull. The lower stringer is the support for the beams that hold the deck while the upper stringer supports the thwarts. The deck in this class of boat is parallel to the waterline and is normally positioned at a level of 3 or 3½ feet below the upper height of the gunwale at midships. Pencil marks are then made at the correct level on the inside of the timbers. This is one of the most difficult stages of building. A piece of wood ¼ inch by ¼ inch is cut so that the length equals the height from the top of the keel to the position of the underside of the deck, as measured on the sheer plan at its lowest point. The plans for *Silver Harvest* do not indicate the position of the deck but in an open boat of this size the upper surface of the deck would be 3 or 3½ inches below the lowest point of the gunwale, at about amidships. With the wooden post vertical and resting on the upper surface of the keel, cut another piece of wood so that when placed horizontally on the top of the post, its ends meet the inside of the hull. A pencil mark is then made on the inside of the hull, representing where the upper edge of the deck stringer is to be fastened. This process now needs to be repeated towards the bow and the stern at intervals of 3 inches or so.

Plate 18. Hull with breasthooks and wales fitted.

Plate 19. Timbers, or ribs, in position.

The stringer that supports the thwarts is positioned ½ inch below the gunwale amidships and stays at this distance below the gunwale, and similar pencil marks are made to show where this stringer will fit. A length of ¼ inch square wood is then fitted along these pencil marks and glued and dowelled in position (Plate 20).

The next task is to fit two mast steps to the keel. Boats from 1850, and of the size of this boat, had two or even three masts each of a length almost equal to that of the keel and in this boat the mast steps are positioned nine and 19 feet (inches at the scale of this model) back from the bow. Blocks of wood, shaped to cover the keel and the adjoining strakes, and drilled to receive half the width of the foot of the mast are formed and fitted at the appropriate points on the keel (Plates 21 and 22).

Beams to support the deck are then cut and fitted across the width of the hull over the lower stringers at every second frame, and supported by pieces of ¼ by ¾ inch baulkes of wood glued to the keel and having a slot cut at the upper end to receive the deck beam. Additional beams need to be fitted on either side of the position of the mast steps to support the mast trunk (Plate 23).

Planking the deck

The deck planks can now be fitted. Lengths of ½ by $^1/_{16}$ inch wood are cut with the circular saw from lime wood and sanded well. The deck planks would have been caulked and a realistic impression of caulking can be made by clamping together six or so lengths of deck planking, spreading a thin layer of glue over one edge of the clamped planks, and fitting the assembly onto a piece of black sugar paper (Plate 24). Once the glue has set the individual planks are separated from each other and from the sugar paper by a razor blade and thus each plank has one edge covered in a thin strip of black paper.

Plate 20. Timbers, stringers and mast steps fitted.

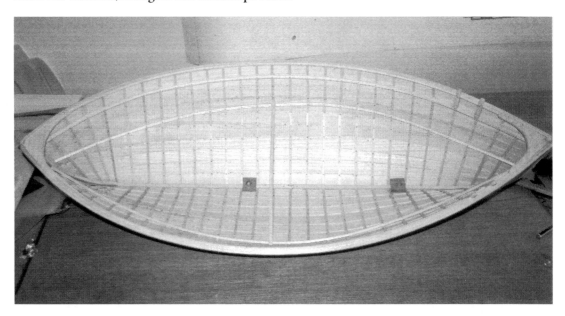

Plate 21. Timbers, stringers and aft mast step.

Plate 22. Forward mast step.

Plate 23. Deck beams and keel supports.

Before the deck can be planked, the inside of the hull from the lower stringer to the gunwale needs to be painted; once this has been done the deck planking can be started. Each plank is, as ever, glued and dowelled to the deck beams with a slot being left over the mast steps set on the keel at the angle required to ensure that whatever rake the mast has will be held in position by the trunk. The arrangement of the deck beams around the position of the mast steps has been particularly chosen so that the trunks that hold the masts at deck level are supported by deck beams (Plates 25 and 26).

Plate 24. Making caulking for deck planks.

Plate 25. Deck planks being laid and fastened.

Plate 26. Planking the deck.

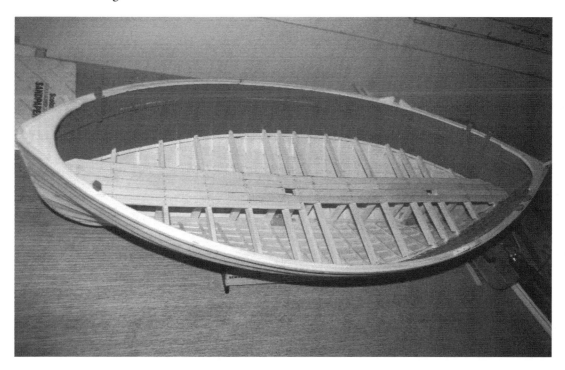

Making the cradle

It is now the appropriate stage to make the cradle that will support the finished boat. Two station lines are selected from the body plan, roughly six inches apart and relatively central to the length of the model. An outline of these two frames is drawn from the body plan, a 1/4 inch cut is drawn at the base of the frame to house the keel and the shape is designed to complete the outline of the stand, with a cut along each lateral side to take a lengthwise plank of wood to hold the ends of the cradle (Plate 27). The name of the boat, its class and its date of origin will eventually be inscribed on the two lateral planks of the cradle.

Mast trunks, thwarts & bilge pump

Once the deck has been completed (Plate 28), a framework of ⅛ by ¹/₁₆ inch wood is glued and dowelled round the openings for the masts, and the thwarts are cut and fastened with the knees reaching along the top of the upper stringer. The mast trunks are constructed in ¹/₁₆ inch wood and extend from the openings in the deck for the masts to the thwarts (Plate 28). The mast trunk is supported forward by a shaped piece of wood and aft by a piece of brass rod. Forward of the mast trunk is another u-shaped piece of brass rod on which a hook has been fitted: this is the 'horse' that takes the tack of the sail (Plate 29; Plate 30).

Plate 27. The form of the cradle.

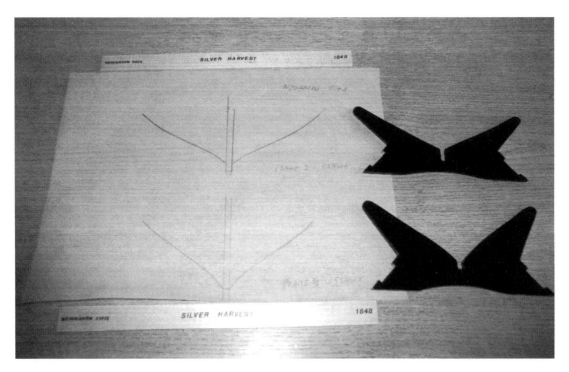

Plate 28. Deck planked with mast openings.

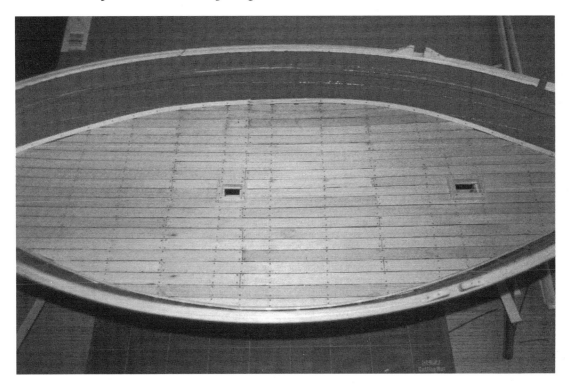

Plate 29. Midships thwart and mast trunk fitted.

Plate 30. Completed mast trunk.

Knees are then fitted vertically between the upper and outer ends of the thwarts and the underside of the in-wale (Plate 31), and these are then glued and dowelled in position. A fully decked boat of this size would need to have a bilge pump, as it would be impossible otherwise to keep the boat free of rain or sea water. Plate 32 shows the housing for the pump with the pump assembly; this is fitted immediately forward of the central thwart of the boat. A hole is drilled at one side of the casing, of a diameter to take a length of ⅛ inch brass tubing, and a length of tubing is then carried from the pump housing to exit through the hull close below the thwart (Plate 33).

Hull fittings

The two projections of the timbers at the bow were probably used to secure the ends of the drift net ropes, since once the nets had been set the boat would lie to them, bow into wind or tide, and drift with the currents overnight. This is the origin of the phrase 'drift net fishing'. Astern of these reinforced timbers are a pair of shaped blocks of wood on either side of the boat, which at first sight seem to be fittings for oars (Plate 33). It is likely that these fittings served as guides for the head rope of the line of drift nets, which were hauled over the gunwale at the end of the night's fishing. These fittings are made of ¼ inch wood and glued and pinned to the top of the rail.

Plate 31. Knees fitted to thwarts.

Plate 32. Pump assembly.

Plate 33. Pump and exit pipe fitted.

The shape of the rudder is drawn from the plans and copied onto wood ¼ inch thick. Once the shape has been cut out using the vibrating saw the rearward edge of the rudder has to be paired away until the edge of the blade is sharp. This is done initially with the craft knife or a drum sander but the final shaping of the rudder needs to be done with sandpaper and lots of elbow grease. The rudder is fitted with pintails, downward-facing posts of brass rod that are housed in the gudgeons, pieces of brass tubing fitted on the sternpost to allow the rudder to turn freely.

To make the pintails, two small pieces of wood, measuring ¼ by ¼ inch, are cut and a groove to accommodate half the diameter of a brass rod is filed on one edge. In this boat the diameter of the brass pintails is $^1/_{16}$ inch and brass tubing has been selected to take that diameter of post. The brass post is cut and glued to the groove in the wooden block with ultra-fast-setting glue, and the assembly is then glued to the rudder. Repeat the process for the lower pintail. Short lengths of brass strip are then cut, drilled, glued and fastened to the rudder with brass nails ¼ inch long. The nails are then doubly secured with a drop of ultra-fast-setting glue (Plate 34).

The gudgeons are made in a similar way with brass tubing replacing the brass rods of the pintails. The gudgeons are also secured to the stern post with lengths of brass strip, nails and ultra-fast-setting glue. The tiller, which has a slot cut into it to take the head of the rudder, is then cut from ¼ inch wood, shaped and sanded, and coloured with Colron Danish Oil™. The deck, deck fittings and thwarts would have needed some protective coating and as varnish quickly becomes discoloured by water seeping under the skin, oil of some kind was used. Danish Oil gives a lovely brown sheen to the wood, and has been used in *Silver Harvest* for these fittings.

Plate 34. The rudder and tiller fitted to the sternpost.

In the latter part of the nineteenth century most boats had cleats fitted to take the various ropes of the rigging but many boats at both an earlier and later time had vertical posts set into the thwarts round which ropes were secured. Belaying pins made of soft wood dowel tend eventually to break off but dowels of the required diameter, ⅛ to ¹⁄₁₆ inch, made from bamboo cane are extremely strong and this wood has been used whenever a boat is fitted with belaying pins rather than cleats (Plate 33).

Rowlocks were a relatively late invention and virtually all boats in the nineteenth century had sets of two thole pins to house the shaft of the oar. These are simply made by attaching with glue and dowels to the top of the rail a pad of wood into which two dowels are fitted. The dowels should project about ½ inch above the rail and be separated by an interval of ½ inch. As with the belaying pins, the thole pins are best made from dowels of bamboo cane.

Oars are made from ¼ inch wood. The four oars for *Silver Harvest* are 18 inches in length with a blade of 4 inches in length. The outline of the oar is drawn on and cut from ¼ inch sheet and the blade is shaped using either the craft knife and sandpaper, or the orbital sander and sandpaper. Only the approximate shape of the blade is cut mechanically; the greater part of the shaping is done using differing grades of sandpaper. The shaft, which after the initial cut is square, ¼ by ¼ inch, is rounded using a craft plane and then sheet after sheet of sandpaper. A rope is wound round the shaft of the oar where it meets the thole pins, and the finished oar is painted with Danish Oil.

Masts and spars

The two masts and the two spars are made from commercial hardwood dowel, the masts from dowel of ½ inch diameter and the spars from dowel of ³/16 inch diameter. The masts are 30 inches in length, the spar for the foremast 14 inches, and the spar for the main mast 18 inches.

The masts need to be tapered but, before this is done, a slot measuring ½ by ⅛ inch needs to be cut through the centre of the dowel two inches from one end. This is achieved by marking the outline of the slot in pencil, drilling a hole the correct diameter at top and bottom of the slot and using the craft knife and a flat file to shape the slot. This slot will house the sheave, the round brass pulley around which the spar up-haul rope will pass.

The mast is tapered using the miniature plane and sandpaper. Starting a quarter of the way from the end of the dowel that has the slot – the upper end of the mast – make one passage of the plane, then repeat this from half-way along the spar to the end, then from three-quarters along the shaft and then from the base end. Repeat this process on all four sides of the mast, and then along the four sharp corners produced by the first four planings. The final shaping of the mast is then achieved by sanding with coarse and then finer papers.

Shaping the spars is slightly different from shaping the masts although the same process is used. Towards one end of the spar a rounded block of wood, drilled with a hole to receive the hook of the up-haul, will be glued and dowelled, and the position of this fitting is 3½ inches from one end of the spar (Plate 35). The position of this fitting is where the spar's thickness is greatest so that the tapering of the two ends of the spar start from a position 3½ inches from one end. Once the spar has been tapered, a hole is drilled ¼ inch from each end to take the rope fittings for the sail, and the up-haul fitting is then made, glued and dowelled, sanded and covered by a narrow band of brass strip. The up-haul fitting and the holes that have been drilled at either end of the spar must be in the same plane. The spars and masts can now be stained with Danish Oil.

The two yards are hoisted up the mast with a fitting called a parrel (Plate 36). A piece of brass rod ¹/32 inch in diameter is formed into a curve about ¼ inch in circumference wider than the diameter of the mast at deck height. Small wooden beads, parrel beads, which can be obtained from craft shops, are then threaded onto the brass ring;

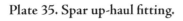

Plate 35. Spar up-haul fitting.

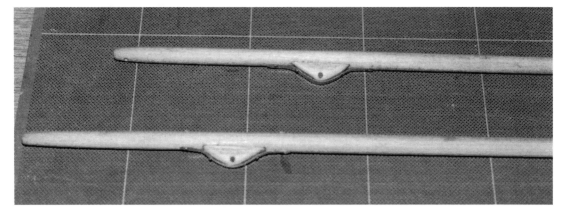

these allow the fitting to be 'run' up the mast without causing damage by the friction of the metal band on the wooden mast. A piece of wood ½ inch long, ¼ inch wide and $^1/_{16}$ inch thick is drilled with a hole the diameter of the rigging rope towards the upper end, and a hole equal to the diameter of the brass ring at midpoint. A third hole of the same diameter as the ring is then drilled part way into the bottom end of the piece of wood. This last will hold the hook that lifts the yard, while the middle hole is incorporated into the parrel ring, with the head rope being fastened to the upper hole.

Plate 36. Parrel fitting.

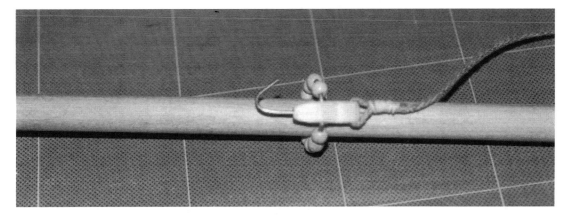

Water barrel & bucket

Boats of this and later vintage generally carried a water barrel, roped to a cradle and positioned either near the bow or towards the stern (Plate 37). To make the barrel cut three round disks of $^1/_{16}$ inch wood, two of 1 inch diameter and the third of 1⅛ inch in diameter. With the two smaller disks positioned in the middle of the larger disk, drill three holes of ⅛ inch diameter through the disks at positions 12, 4 and 8 o'clock. Thread three 1¾ inch lengths of ⅛ inch dowel through the holes so that the smaller pieces are at each end with the larger disk in the centre. This will now give the natural shape of the barrel. Cut a number of lengths of wood ¼ inch wide and $^1/_{32}$ inch thick, taper the ends from the mid-point with the miniature plane, fit each one over the curve of the barrel and fix in position with glue and a very narrow dowel (Plate 38; Plate 39). When the barrel is finished sand it down and drill a ¼ inch hole at the centre of the uppermost part of the barrel—this will be fitted with a wooden plug. At the lowest point of one end of the barrel drill a hole, $^1/_{16}$ inch in diameter, drill a smaller hole through the end of a piece of $^1/_{16}$ inch brass tubing and fit the short piece of tubing into the hole in the barrel to form the outlet. A small wooden handle is then made, drilled at one end with a $^1/_{32}$ inch bit; the handle is then secured to the outlet pipe with a bamboo dowel.

A small wooden cradle, similar to the boat cradle, is made and horizontal holes, $^1/_{16}$ inch in diameter, are drilled through the lower points of the 'legs' of the cradle, and the barrel is then fastened to the cradle with rope. To secure the barrel and cradle to the deck, drill angled holes through the outward ends of the cradle and through the deck planking, and fasten with glue and dowels.

Plate 37. Water barrel.

The wooden bucket is made in a very much similar way. Two disks of $^1/_{16}$ inch wood are cut, one 1 inch in diameter and the other $^1/_8$ inch in diameter smaller. The smaller disk is then glued in the centre of the larger disk to form the base of the bucket. A number of strips of wood are cut, $^1/_8$ inch wide by $^1/_{16}$ inch thick. Two strips, which will take the rope carrying-handle, are cut $^1/_4$ inch longer than the others and have a hole drilled in the upper end. The two longer pieces of wood are glued into the shelf formed by the two disks, opposite each other, and the other, shorter, strips of wood are then bevelled on each side and fitted and glued round the circumference of the bucket. The completed bucket is sanded down, stained and then fitted with a rope handle (Plate 40).

Plate 38. Carcase and staves of the water barrel.

Plate 39. Construction of water barrel.

Plate 40. Wooden bucket.

Rigging

Fishing boats of the early nineteenth century had the minimum of standing rigging and the feature that made this possible was the mast trunk. The mast was bedded into a mast step fitted to the keel for strength, and three or more feet above this the mast was held securely in a trunk, constructed of heavy lengths of wood and made even more secure by sturdy wedges to keep the mast from moving in any direction. The mast trunk of *Silver Harvest* can be seen in Plate 30.

Larger boats, such as the Zulus of the late nineteenth century with keels 70 feet long, required more standing rigging although the principle of a strong mast trunk to support the mast at gunwale height was kept. *Silver Harvest* achieves additional support for the mast by having the yard up-hauls secured to belaying pins on the windward side, the side opposite to where the sail has been set.

In this model good quality rigging cord of about 2 mm diameter has been used; rigging cords of various diameters are readily obtained from model shops. The blocks were bought commercially but this supplier has unfortunately gone out of business and, in future, blocks, either single or double, complete with sheaves and served with brass wire will have to be made locally.

Sails are made from sail cloth, again obtained from model shops, and dyed a dark brown to represent the age-old custom of 'barking' the nets and sails with tree bark to preserve the cotton fabric against salt and sea spray. It is important that an accurate drawing is made of the dimensions of each of the boat's sails. The sails of boats of the nineteenth century were generally what are called 'dipping lug sails'. The upper length of sail was attached to the yard and when set lay at about 45 degrees to the mast. The forward edge of the sail led down to, in this instance, a hook on a length of chain attached to the traveller positioned in the thwart forward of the mast. The foot of the sail was free and the sail would have three lines of reefing ropes, across the sail, and marked at the aft border of the sail by three rings sewn into the edge of the sail. If the sail was reefed, the sheet was then moved to the ring that was in line with, now, the lower edge of the sail.

It is thus important to hold the yard in its eventual position and to measure accurately the shape and dimensions of the sail. A length of rigging cord needs to be sewn into the forward and upper edges of the sail, while on the upper length, where it will be fastened to the yard, a number of rings have to be sewn into the sail at each end and at intervals of one inch along the length. The upper border of the sail is fastened to the yard by a length of rigging cord attached to the hole in the yard and passed through the rings on the upper border of the sail and round the yard (Plate 41).

The final addition to the boat should always be at least one replica fisherman, since the inclusion of a scale figure means that the length and other dimensions of the boat are instantly apparent. Ideally the number of 'fishermen' should be the same as the original crew, in the case of *Silver Harvest* probably three or four in number. Models of very realistic dolls, with movable limbs, at a scale of 1 : 12 can be obtained commercially at a very reasonable cost. The dolls need only to be dressed in a sweater and trousers, although greater effect can be had by dressing each doll differently and positioning them as if they were at their proper tasks in the boat (Plate 42).

Plate 41. Sails.

Plate 42. *Silver Harvest.*

CHAPTER 5: BUILDING A CARVEL-HULLED DECKED BOAT

Carvel-built boats really only appeared in the Northeast fisheries in the latter half of the nineteenth century, when the development of deep-water harbours, where boats could lie afloat against a harbour wall, changed the fishing scene and, in particular, the size and design of fishing boats.

Unlike a clench-built boat, the hull of which is constructed upside down and gets its strength from the overlap, or 'lands', between the lower edge of one plank and the upper edge of the next, a carvel-built hull obtains its strength from closely spaced, heavy frames. The hull strakes abut edge to edge and can be of any convenient length since the vertical butt edges of adjoining strakes are fastened to a frame. This method of construction thus allowed much larger craft to be built than was possible where the strake had to run in one piece between the bow and the stern post.

The model used to illustrate this form of building is a Fifie, registration number BK 918, which sailed from Burnmouth and was photographed in her home port in 1882 (Plate 43). She was of an unusual construction in that the original boat was clench built over frames. Her keel length was 38 feet, 6 inches with a waterline of 42 feet. Plans of a 1905 carvel-built St. Monance Fifie, *True Vine*, drawn from the original boat by Phillip Oke in 1936 were used for the hull construction and adapted so that the keel length was 38½ inches (Figures 14, 15 & 16).

As with a clench-built boat, a building board is required and the length and width of the keel are marked along the midline of the board along with the positions of the station lines, taken from the half-breadth plan The half-breadth plan has a total of 13 station lines, six in the stern half of the boat and seven in the bow section. This means that frames, constructed to represent the station lines as seen in the body plan, would be, in the model, about 3 inches apart. Additional lines thus need to be drawn on the body plan midway between the existing 13 lines to form additional station lines, and thus the position of new frames. On the half-breadth plan, these will add another 14 station lines positioned midway between the existing lines and between the bow and stern and their adjacent station lines.

Plate 43. The Burnmouth Fifie BK 918 in 1882.

The keel, stemhead, sternpost and deadwoods are all taken off the sheer plan with tracing paper and using carbon paper are drawn on to ½ inch thick lime or bass wood. The keel may need to be in two equal sections, as it can be difficult to obtain wood of this length; if two pieces are used, they need to be joined with a scarf and fastened together with glue and wooden dowels. A scarf joint is rather like a 'Z' shape (Figure 1) and ensures a strong joint between the two lengths of wood. The stem and stern posts should be cut to their precise lengths and not left 1 inch longer as is necessary with a clench-built boat, since a carvel-built hull is constructed with the keel downwards.

Figure 1. A scarf joint.

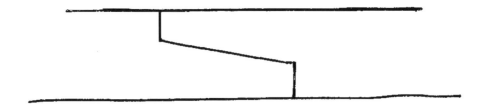

The stem and stern posts (Figure 2) and the deadwoods are glued and dowelled in place. After this a rabbet is cut along the lengths of the stem and stern posts and along the keel, leaving ½ inch from the lower side of the keel rabbet to the bottom side of the keel. The complete keel assembly can now be fitted into the building frame: the stem and stern posts are held between the upward arms of angle irons screwed into the building board while small blocks of wood screwed to the board on either side of the keel line at intervals of about six inches give lateral support to the keel. The keel assembly should fit neatly, as a push fit, into the angle irons and keel side supports and be thus held rigidly in place.

Figure 2. Stem and stern posts.

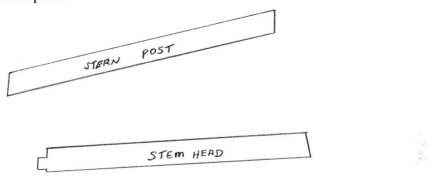

Building the frames

The construction of the frames is perhaps the most difficult part of building a carvel hull, not so much in the middle and forward part of the boat, but towards the stern where the external shape of the hull becomes concave and can change in shape considerably. It is thus necessary to cut frames in thin plywood where there is any significant alteration in hull shape, fit them to the keel and, if a length of wood strip does not then lie closely against all of the frames, the curve of the temporary frame can be corrected until the 'strake' lies accurately in contact with the frames.

Each frame is in three parts, one that extends across the keel to the sides of the hull and thus forms the floor on which the lower deck will be laid, and two 'arms' that extend up to the level of the gunwale (Figure 3). This allows the grain in the wood to lie on the long axis of the part. The outline of the ½ inch keel width is drawn on tracing paper and then, using a flexible ruler, the appropriate lines of the 'arm' on one side are drawn from the body plan. The tracing paper then needs to be turned over so that the other side of the frame can be drawn from the same line on the body plan. On the tracing paper the upper side of the base of the frame is drawn to form the floors, and a line, ¼ inch in width, is marked parallel to and inside the 'arms' of the frame. The position of the overlap of the base and the 'arms' of the frame are then marked, and the resultant three parts of the frame are transferred to ¼ inch bass or lime wood with carbon paper.

Once the three parts of each frame are cut and sanded, a ½ by ¼ inch slot is cut into the base part where it will fit over the keel, and the parts are glued and dowelled in position, using the outline of the frame, on the tracing paper, as a guide. The frames

Figure 3. Outline of a typical frame.

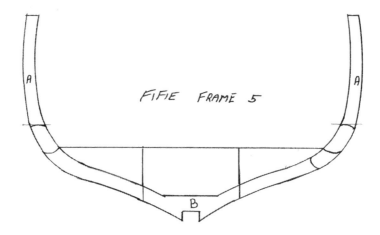

in the centre of the hull will have a square outline to the 'arms', but suceeding frames, as they come to lie more and more towards the bow or the stern, need to be shaped to follow the curve of the gunwale and hull. This is most necessary in the 'arms', less so at the base of the frame, and the angling of the inward and outward sides of the 'arms' is achieved by paring the edges with a craft knife and then finishing the slope off with sandpaper. This angling of the sides of the frames ensures that the strakes – and the inward stringers and the inwale – lie closely against the sides of the frames as they reach from bow to stern.

In this boat, as in most designs of this time, the 'arms' of the first two bow frames are continued above the level of the gunwale by 1 inch. These extensions acted as the posts to which the end rope of the length of drift netting was fastened while the boat lay to her nets overnight.

Once all the 30 or so frames have been made – and it is important to remember that the frames towards the bow and stern of the boat need to have a cut in the base over the keel that can accommodate the height and slope of the deadwoods as well as the keel – the frames can be glued and dowelled to the keel. It is very important to ensure that the frames are positioned vertical to the keel and precisely at right angles to the sides of the keel (Plates 44 & 45).

It would be very difficult to plank the hull with the frames only supported at their base by glue and dowels, so a permanent or temporary outwale needs to be fastened to the frame heads to support them while the strakes are fastened in position. It is probably best to make the outwale a temporary fitting using a strip of ¼ by ⅛ inch wood since the use of a thin strip of wood means that the process of curving the strakes round the frame heads will not distort their positions relative to the stem and stern posts. This temporary outwale can be pinned to the bow and stern posts and fastened to the frame heads with clothes pegs or clamps. This temporary outwale will in time be replaced by a permanent wale.

The hull now has an early resemblance to a boat. The skeleton is the correct way up, the keel, stem and stern posts are in position and the frames and the outwale show the curve of the hull and of the gunwale. All that needs to be done is to fit the strakes and the hull will be complete.

Plates 44. The keel assembly with frames set up.

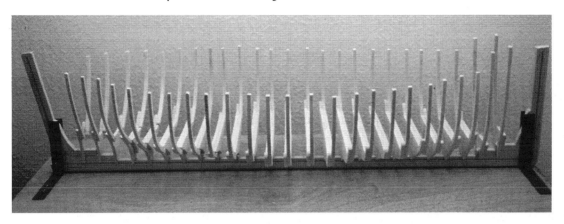

Plate 45. Frames fitted to keel.

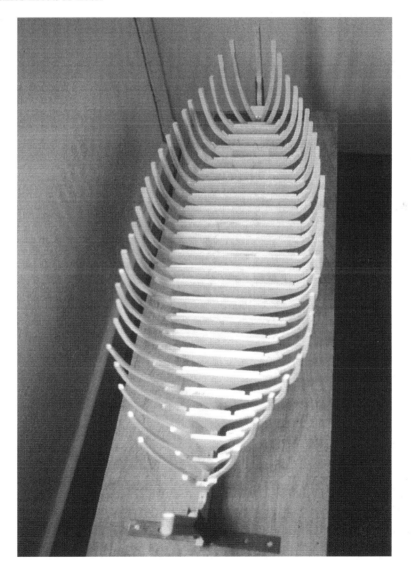

Fitting the lower deck

Longitudinal pieces of strip wood, ⅛ by ¼ inch, need to be fitted from bow to stern to support the lower and upper decks and the upper edges of these stringers need to be shaped so that they lie horizontal despite the curves of the hull (Plates 46, 47, 48 & 49). In this small Fifie the lower stringers are not required since the lower deck is fitted directly onto the frame floors. The floors are 3½ inches below the lowest point of the gunwale at midships and are parallel to the keel. The supports for the upper deck are fitted 1 inch below and parallel to the gunwale. The stringers are glued and dowelled to the frames.

In some designs the mast steps are fastened directly on to the keel but occasionally, as in this boat, the mast steps are fitted directly to the lower deck. In the former arrangement the positions of the two mast steps need to be marked on the keel and blocks of ½ inch thick wood are drilled to give a depression ¼ inch in diameter that will receive the cut-down foot of the mast. The blocks are shaped to fit over the keel and lie against the sides of the hull and are then glued and dowelled in position. When the mast step is fitted to the lower deck, rather than directly onto the keel, the block needs to be glued and dowelled to the deck with reinforcing baulkes of wood, ¼ by ¼ inch, round the outside of the mast step. The forward mast is approximately one fifth of the length of the boat back from the bow and rakes slightly astern while the mizzen mast step is at about one third of the length of the boat from the stern and is angled forward.

The lower deck is fitted first. Unless the lower deck is fitted directly to the frame floors as in this model, beams of ¼ inch square wood are cut and fastened so that they lie across the hull from the upper end of the lower stringer on one side to the same position on the opposite stringer, at each second frame. The beams should be given the additional support of a baulk of wood, ½ x ¼ inch, fitted from the upper side of the keel to the underside of the beam and notched to form a 'U' shape around the base and sides of the beam. Additional beams are fitted around the exit site of the masts so that each mast has a beam at either side, fore and aft, on which the mast trunk can be constructed.

Before any further work can be done it is necessary to seal the interior of the hull with a matt varnish or oil-based sealant such as Danish Oil™ from the position of the lower deck beams to the upper edge of the gunwale. Avoid getting any sealant on the upper edges of the stringers for the lower and upper decks. Two coats of sealant are applied, with the first coat being sanded down before the second is applied.

Using the circular saw, lengths of ½ by ⅛ inch wood are cut to form the deck planks. These planks can either be continuous or in two or more sections and are 'caulked' using black sugar paper. Starting at the mid point of the deck, and obviously interrupting the planking if mast exit sites are present, the deck planks are fitted, glued and dowelled to the transverse beams.

Fitting the strakes

Since the hull of this boat is only 42 feet long at the most, it might be practical and possible to have the individual strakes each of the length needed to reach from the bow to the stern post. In a larger carvel-built boat, however, this would be impossible, so each length of hull planking would be in two or more sections. The vertical edges of the

Plate 46. Outwale, breast hooks, upper deck stringer and lower deck assembled.

Plate 47. Stern section.

Plate 48. Bow section.

Plate 49. Bow section: lower deck and outwale fitted.

individual strakes need to meet at a frame and be fastened to it and there were, in the late nineteenth century, very precise guidelines as to the positioning of strake butt ends on the frames: "No butts to be nearer that 5 ft. of each other unless there be a strake wrought between them, in which case a distance of 4 ft. will be allowed. No butts to be on the same timber (frame) unless there be three strakes between them."

With this model of a small Fifie, however, the greatest strake length is 42 inches and, since this length of timber can be obtained as a single length, the strakes of this model will reach from stern to stem. Planking of the hull can start at the outwale or at the garboard strake at the keel but it is probably more convenient to start at the upper end of the frames. As with the clench-built boat, the number of strakes on each side needs to be decided and, using the proportional dividers, a mark made with pencil to show the position of the lower end of each strake on every second frame and on the stem and stern posts.

The first strake is cut larger than the greatest width of the strake and then bent round the frames with the upper edge shaped to accommodate to the curve of the hull at the outwale. The width of the strake is then marked at each frame so that a curving line can be drawn through the points and the strake is then cut along this line. Since this is a carvel built hull there is no need to shape the lower one inch length of the strake at the bow and stern: the strakes lie edge on to each other and do not overlap.

Planking then continues, individual strakes being glued and dowelled to the frames and to the stern and stem posts, held in place while glueing with clothes pegs. The hull assembly can be lifted out of the building jig when the last two or so strakes need to be fastened, and the planked hull can then be sanded down and finished. The temporary outwale, if that was what was used, is now removed and the permanent outwale is fitted (Plate 50).

Plate 50. The hull planked.

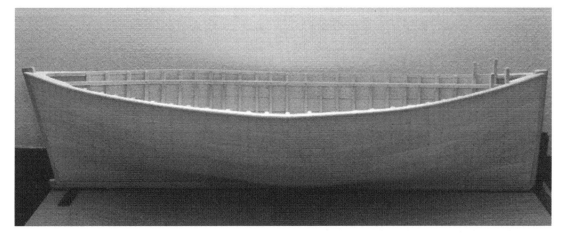

The stringers and carlings of the upper deck

The supports for the upper deck are complex since they need to allow in the bow section for the mast trunk, the hatch to the fo'c'sle cabin and a longitudinal slot that carries a removable board that, when in position, braces the aft side of the main mast (Plate51); at the stern there is an opening where the net and head rope were stowed (Plate52). In the centre of the upper deck is a large longitudinal opening into which the catch was dropped down to the lower deck (Plate 53).

Plate 51. Bow supports for upper deck.

Plate 52. Upper deck supports at stern, with main mast crutch.

Plate 53. Upper deck supports.

The mast trunk now needs to be constructed and fitted once the various upper deck stringers and carlings have been glued in position (Plate 54). The trunk for the mizzen mast can be seen in Plate 55 as the lower opening astern of the main opening into the fish-hold. The square slot in the adjacent upper block is for the main mast crutch, onto which the main mast was lowered while the boat was lying to the nets overnight.

Plate 54. Upper deck fittings.

Plate 55. Close-up of upper deck fittings.

The vertical supports for the fish-hold beams, the sides of the various openings in what will be the upper deck, the main mast trunk and the opening for the net head rope at the stern of the boat now need to be painted before the upper deck is laid. A ring needs to be fastened to the lower part of the stem post to which is attached the anchor chain since, once the upper deck is in position, it will be impossible to drill and fasten the chain ring. The chain will be led through a hole drilled in the upper deck and secured with a safety pin pending later attachment to the anchor (Plate 56). The state of the boat can now be seen in Plates 57 and 58.

Plate 56. Bow section of boat.

Plate 57. Boat upper deck supports.

Plate 58. Hull planked, wales and rubbing strakes fastened, partially decked.

Once the upper deck has been laid it is time to make and fit the deck fittings, the thwarts, cleats and other fastenings. Plates 59 and 60 show the inwale attached to the frame heads, the stern thwart, cleats and the net roller and its fittings. The fitting on the stern thwart to take the heel of the bumkin is made from brass strip and the rudder and tiller are drawn from the plans and cut in ¼ inch thick wood (Figure 4). The rudder gudgeons and pintails are made with brass rod and strip as has been described for the clench-built boat and this now essentially completes the construction of the hull (Plate 61).

Plate 59. Stern of the boat, with deck laid and net roller fitted.

Plate 60. Completed bow section of boat.

Figure 4. Drawing of rudder and tiller.

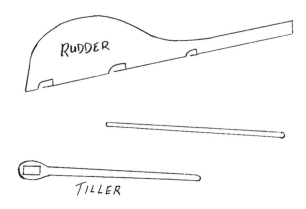

Plate 61. The completed Burnmouth Fifie.

CHAPTER 6: INTERNAL EQUIPMENT FOR MODEL FISHING BOATS

After the boat has been built another and equally interesting phase starts: designing and making the fishing equipment that the boat might have carried. In this, the imagination can run riot but, although the internal equipment of the boat can add realism to the model, the addition of sails and one or more dressed and appropriate dolls at the required scale gives the model a life that the bare hull and fittings fail to convey.

All of my models are equipped with a wooden bucket and water barrel, sometimes rope bound, sometimes with brass bands. Each boat has the appropriate number of oars of the correct length, some of which have a brass band round the lower part of the blade, and, in addition, either thole pins or rowlocks. All recent models have sails and rigging and at least one fisherman in appropriate clothing positioned in the boat to emphasise the scale. In the Scottish Fisheries Museum in Anstruther the model of the 34-foot Shetland haddock boat, *Owners Delight*, was positioned next to the diminutive 18-foot Largs line skiff and, without the benefit of a scale fisherman, it is easy to assume that these two boats have been built to differing scales.

A list, not exhaustive, of the internal fittings of some of the boats illustrated is now appended.

Herring shovel

See Plate 62 (*Gratitude of Portnockie*), Plate 70 (*Bounty*), Plate 81 (*Snowdrop* of Ardrishaig), and Plate 85 (*Brothers*).

Wooden herring shovels were in common use during the latter half of the nineteenth century and are easily reproduced at a 1:12 scale. The advantage that the wooden shovel had over a metal one was that it did not bruise the fish as a metal one might do. And, of course, it was immune to rust.

The outline of the shovel is first drawn on a sheet of ¼-inch basswood, with measurements of 3 inches in total length and 1½ inches as the width of the bottom end of the shovel. The outline of the recessed part of the shovel is then drawn and after cuts of about ³/₁₆-inch have been made with the craft knife across the curved head of the shovel end and the two sides, the 'shovel' end is then carefully cut out using a ¼-inch chisel and sandpaper. Once the shovel end has been completed, three small holes are drilled in the handle and the grip is then cut using the craft knife and needle files. The shovel in its entirety is then cut with the vibrating saw, and the shaft and edges are rounded and smoothed with sandpaper. The completed herring shovel is finally given two coats of Danish oil.

Skim Net

See Plate 63 (*Gratitude of Portnockie*).

The youngest member of the crew, usually a teen-age boy, was given no pay since he was in effect an apprentice. He had as one of his duties the rescue of herring that fell out of the net as it was hauled aboard. Tradition had it that the best herring fell from the net and the skim net was used to retrieve these fish; the rescued fish formed all that the boy received in pay.

The skim net is simply a 10-inch length of dowelling to the top of which is fastened, in grooves, by rope, a brass rod loop 1½ inch in diameter to which an appropriate cone of netting has been attached. The greatest difficulty in making the fitting is not the structure but in finding a source of netting with a mesh that is realistic for a 1:12 model. Perhaps this is why only one of my models is equipped with a skim net.

Fish boxes

See Plate 63 (*Gratitude of Portnockie*), Plate 77 (*Gylen*), Plate 81 (*Snowdrop* of Ardrishaig), Plate 83 (*Jean Morgan*) and Plate 88 (*Dora*).

Fish boxes are easily made using ¹/₁₆-inch wood for the ends and ¹/₃₂-inch wood for the sides and bases. The end panels are drilled for rope handles and the name of the owner of the boat and its port of registration can be 'written' on the side using Letraset stencils.

Forecabin, steam engine, and other fittings for *Owners Delight* and *Bonny Jean*

Owners Delight is fully decked and *Bonny Jean* is half decked and in both boats the fore-cabin is equipped with bunks, made from ¹/₁₆-inch mahogany sheet, a wooden built replica of a stove and a brass outlet vent. The fore-deck of *Owners Delight* was made with a section that could be lifted free, thus allowing the interior of the cabin to be seen.

A picture of a Bolsover steam engine was obtained for *Owners Delight* from an edition of the early 1900s journal, *Model Engineer*. A wooden replica was built with various pieces of brass tubing attached and the final product was an apparently real engine. The grating in the steering well of *Owners Delight*, and the wheel and worm-drive steering system were obtained commercially.

Creels

See Plate 70 (*Bounty*), Plate 81 (*Snowdrop* of Ardrishaig) and Plate 86 (*Brothers*).

The creels were bought commercially: a good source of these and other miniature fittings can be obtained from exhibitions of doll's houses and miniatures and craft fayres.

Hand line

See Plate 72 (*Duncan the Post's boat*).

The hand line is easily made to scale with two shaped sides and dowel cross pieces, and with line or thread wound round the cross pieces. Additional realism can be had by attaching small fishing hooks to the end of the line, and a number of 'fish' can be made from salt-dough, painted and set on deck or in fish boxes. These features can also be added to the long line trays which are included in the models of *Jean Morgan* (Plate 83) and *Snowdrop* of Ardrishaig (Plate 81).

Lobster pot

See Plate 72 (*Duncan the Post's boat*).

The lobster pot was made with a base of $1/16$-inch wood drilled to receive the ends of the curved wooden uprights made from fresh twigs cut in the garden. Being fresh the twigs readily assume the curve of the pot and are glued into the holes in the base. The whole is then covered by miniature netting and, if wished, an entry port can be fastened to the netting with a thin brass ring.

Dan buoy

See Plate 72 (*Duncan the Post's boat*), Plate 81 (*Snowdrop of Ardrishaig*) and Plate 86 (*Brothers*).

The Dan buoy was used to mark the position of lobster pots, a long line of fish hooks or the furthest end of a line of herring drift nets. A conical wooden plug is made of about ¾-inch diameter at its widest part with a $1/16$-inch hole drilled across the wider base and another into the apex. A length of rope attached to a small stone leads down from the lower drilled hole, to which the end of the long line or a head rope for the lobster pot would have been attached. A 3-inch post of $1/16$-inch dowel with a flag attached to the top is inserted into the drilled hole in the apex of the buoy. This would mark the position of the buoy.

CHAPTER 7: PLANS AND DESCRIPTIONS OF BOATS BUILT

East-coast boats of the mid-nineteenth century

The report on the 1848 summer storms that caused such loss of life and the destruction of some 124 fishing boats off the north-east coast of Scotland was prepared by Captain Washington, RN and published by the Government in 1849. It drew attention to a wide diversity of problems in the herring-fishing industry. Repeated mention was made of the paucity of sheltered harbours, the poor maintenance of, and lack of basic equipment at, the few harbours that did exist, all of which contrasted with the immense importance of the industry to the economic life of the north-east, perhaps one of the most economically deprived areas of Scotland.

Accurate plans of every type of fishing boat in use on the north-east coast during the middle of the nineteenth century were included in the *Washington Report*. In contrast to the west coast where a greater variety of smaller boats fished the sea lochs for herring and deeper-swimming fish at other seasons by way of lines rather than nets, on the north-east coast, two distinct types of fishing boat were then in use: the Buckie Scaffie, characterised by a short keel, a rounded fore-foot and a sharply angled stern-post; and the Fifie, with its near vertical stem and stern-posts. The Fifie type tended to show only slight variations in design from port to port as a consequence of the preferences of local builders and fisherfolk.

The Scaffie

The Scaffie had a keel length of 32 to 33 feet but the curve of the bow and the stern-post set at a 45 degree angle increased the overall length to 40 or 41 feet. The maximum beam was generally a third of the overall length and the depth was about 4 feet 9 inches. While the bigger Scaffies fished many miles off-shore, there were many much smaller versions, of 24 feet or so overall length, that never ventured far from their home port. The larger boats had a hull weight of about 3 tons and thus could be readily hauled up a beach to above the high waterline; at sea they carried stone ballast of 1 ton and had a loaded displacement of 16 tons. There were two or even three masts, each of which carried a dipping lug sail, the mizzen stepped at one third of the length from stern to bow with a second mast, of equal height, at about one third of the distance back from the bow to the stern. The normal crew in the large Scaffies comprised at least two men with fishing and sailing experience and another two labourers and a boy. The Scaffie was the preferred design for many years along the Moray Firth and northwards to Wick and, while the boat was good and fast into the wind, the short keel made her relatively unstable downwind and more liable to broach if hit by a quartering sea. The plans of a large Scaffie, taken from the *Washington Report* are shown in Figure 5.

The Fifie

The *Washington Report* also included four sets of plans of Fifies in common use in the first half of the nineteenth century: designs from Wick, Fraserburgh, Peterhead and Newhaven, all of which, while essentially of the same design, show a number of minor variations (Figures 6 to 9). The principal characteristic of the Fifie was the long keel and the almost vertical stem- and stern-posts, which made the boat slow to tack but gave stability downwind. The plans of the Aberdeen boat of 1850 seem almost to be midway between a Scaffie and a Fifie (Figure 10).

The Fifie-type boats, like the Scaffies, had a maximum overall length of about 40 feet. This was partly due to the need to have a relatively light boat that could be pulled to above the high-water line and partly because, as all of these boats were clench built, the length of boat was constrained by the length of continuous planking that could be obtained. All of these boats with the exception of the Fraserburgh boat, which was half decked, were open boats with the main deck lying 3 to 3½ feet below the lowest point of the gunwale. When the *Washington Report* advocated fully decked boats, with the deck 1 foot below the gunwale, the suggestion met with widespread hostility from the fishermen themselves, who maintained that only open boats were suitable for herring fishing and that a deck so close to the gunwale would increase the dangers to men working on deck.

Figure 5. Buckie Scaffie, 1850.

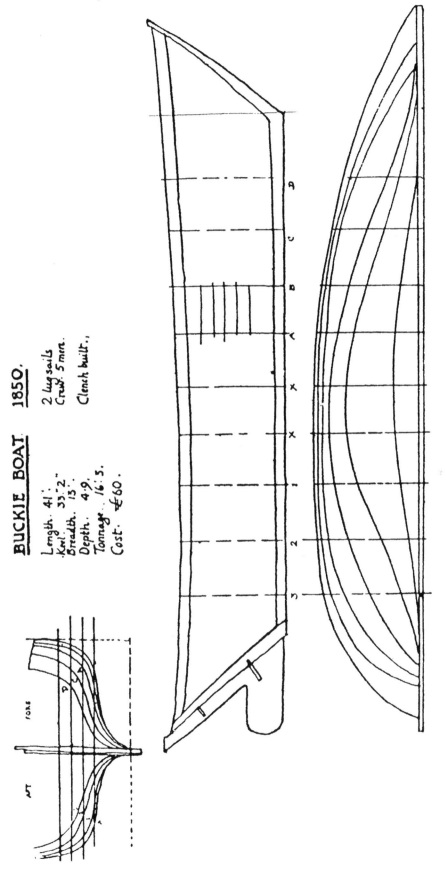

BUCKIE BOAT.   1850.

Length. 41'.   2 lugsails
Kul. 33'-2".   Crew. 5 men.
Breadth. 13'.
Depth. 4'.9.   Clench built.,
Tonnage. 16.5.
Cost. £60.

Figure 6. Wick Boat, 1850.

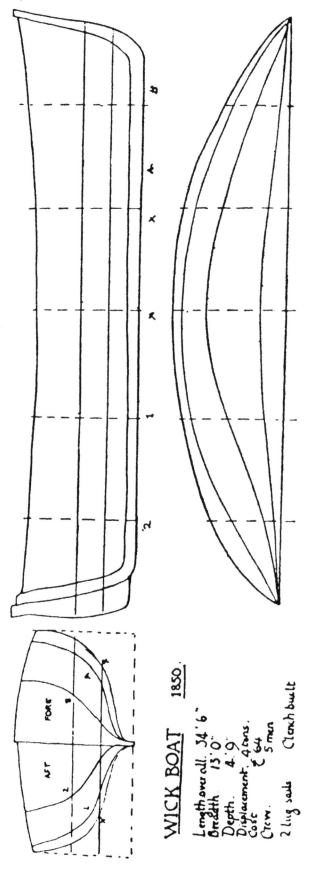

WICK BOAT   1850.

Length overall. 34' 6"
Breadth   13' 0"
Depth   4' 9
Displacement. 4 tons.
Cost   £ 64
Crew.   5 men

2 lug sails   Clinch built

Figure 7. Fraserburgh boat, 1850.

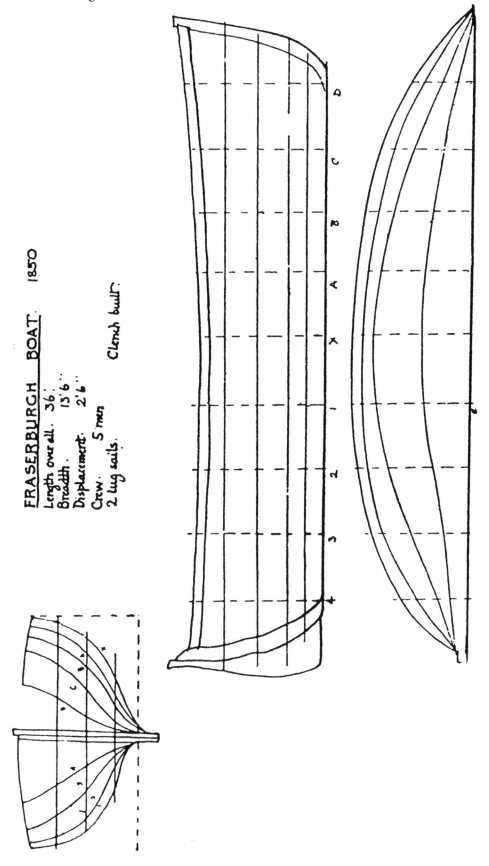

Figure 8. Peterhead boat, 1850.

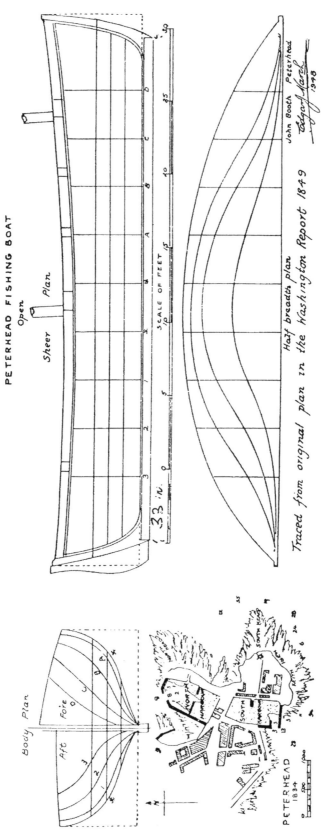

Figure 9. Newhaven Fifie, 1850.

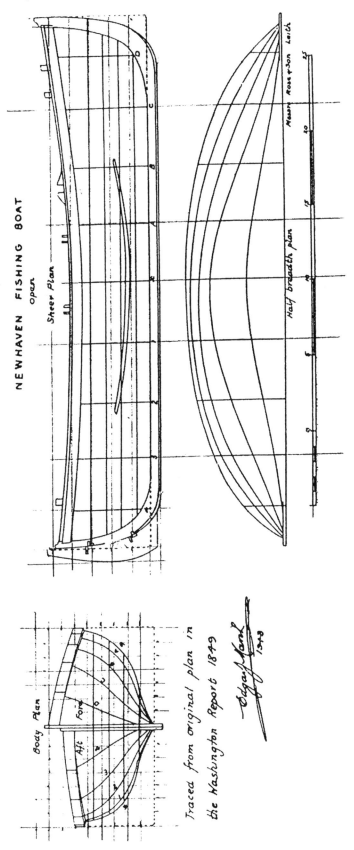

NEWHAVEN FISHING BOAT
open

Sheer Plan

Half breadth plan

Mssrs Ross & Son Leith

Body Plan

Fore

Aft

Traced from original plan in
the Washington Report 1849

Figure 10. Aberdeen boat, 1850.

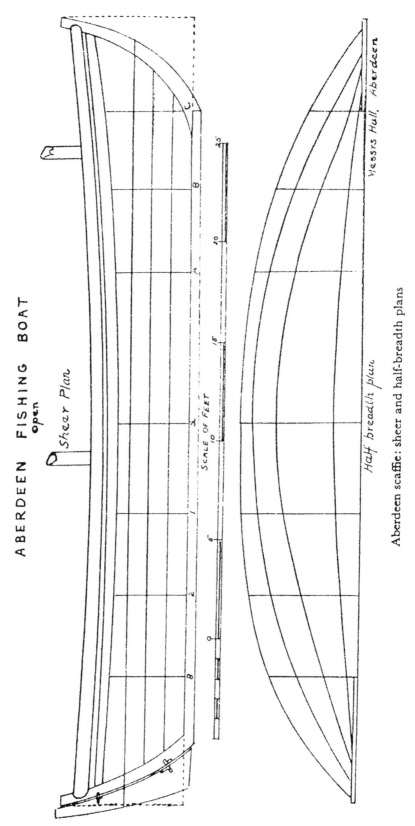

Aberdeen scaffie: sheer and half-breadth plans

Moray Firth Scaffie, *Gratitude* of Portnockie BCK 252

The plans of this boat were drawn by Philip Oke in 1936 and represent a small Scaffie built in 1896 by George Innes of Portnockie, Banffshire, for the owner, Mr. David Mair (Figures 11, 12, & 13). Oke's plans are detailed and show the position of the lower deck, the upper deck laid above the thwarts, the position of the mast step and trunk and indeed all internal fittings. This was a small Scaffie, with a hull length of 24 feet and width of 8 feet 6 inches. The main sail was a dipping lug with a jib positioned on a bowsprit of 13 feet in length.

Photographs of a completed Scaffie, *Gratitude*, built at a scale of 1:12 are shown in Plates 62 & 63.

Plate 62. *Gratitude* **of Portnockie.**

Figure 11. Moray Firth scaffie (lines and sheer plans).

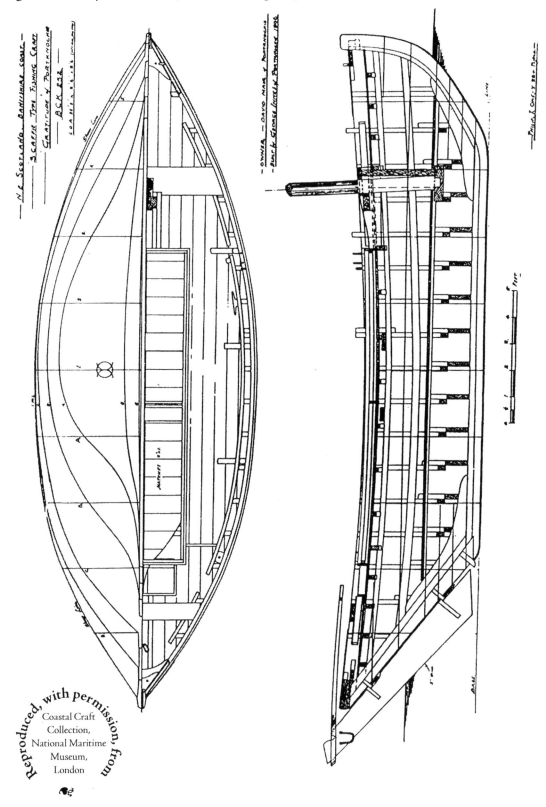

Figure 12. Moray Firth scaffie (body plan).

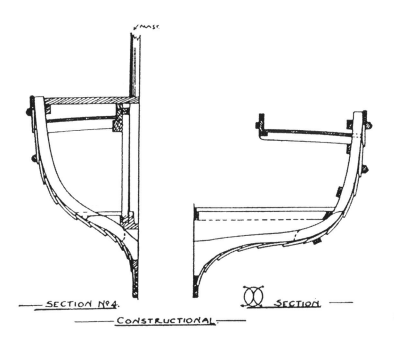

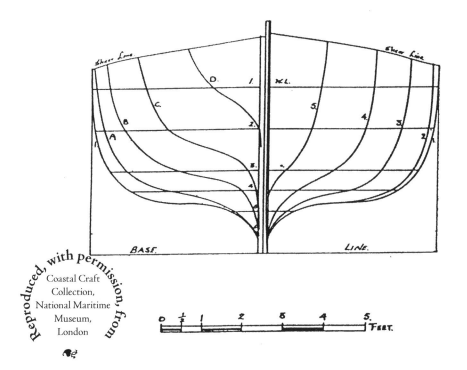

Figure 13. Moray Firth scaffie (sail plan).

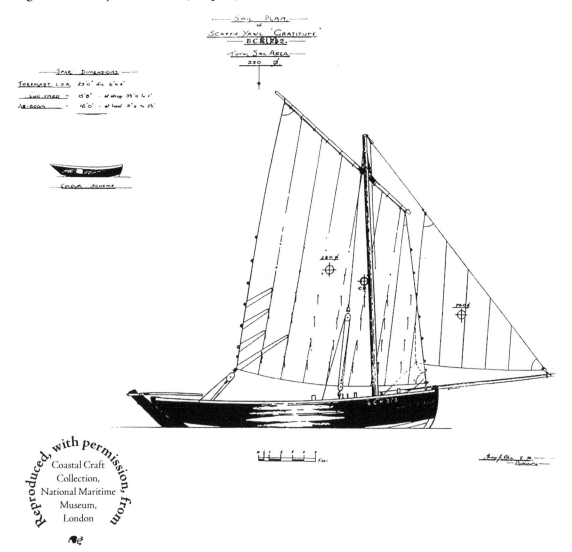

Plate 63. Buckie scaffie, *Gratitude.*

Fifie, *True Vine* ML20

This big Fifie boat, built in 1905 by Robertson Innes at St. Monance, Fife, had a length of 71 feet, breadth of 21 feet and a depth of 8 feet. She weighed 52 tons and was thus obviously intended to remain afloat in harbour rather than to be hauled ashore to above the high-water mark. The plans shown in Figures 14, 15 & 16 were first drawn by Philip Oke and finalised by Edgar March and give considerable detail of the construction of the boat, her lines and her internal fittings.

This was a big boat and, by the standards of her time, a modern and well-equipped vessel. She was carvel built with strakes over heavy frames, and there were crew cabins and a covered fish-hold with the main deck one foot below the level of the gunwale. A steam capstan was used to raise and lower the main mast, which was held in a crutch when lowered; steering was by means of a worm-drive arrangement attached to a wheel rather than a tiller. The sail arrangement comprised main and mizzen dipping lugs with a foresail set on a 40-foot-long bowsprit.

Figure 14: Fifie *True Vine* ML20 (accommodation plan).

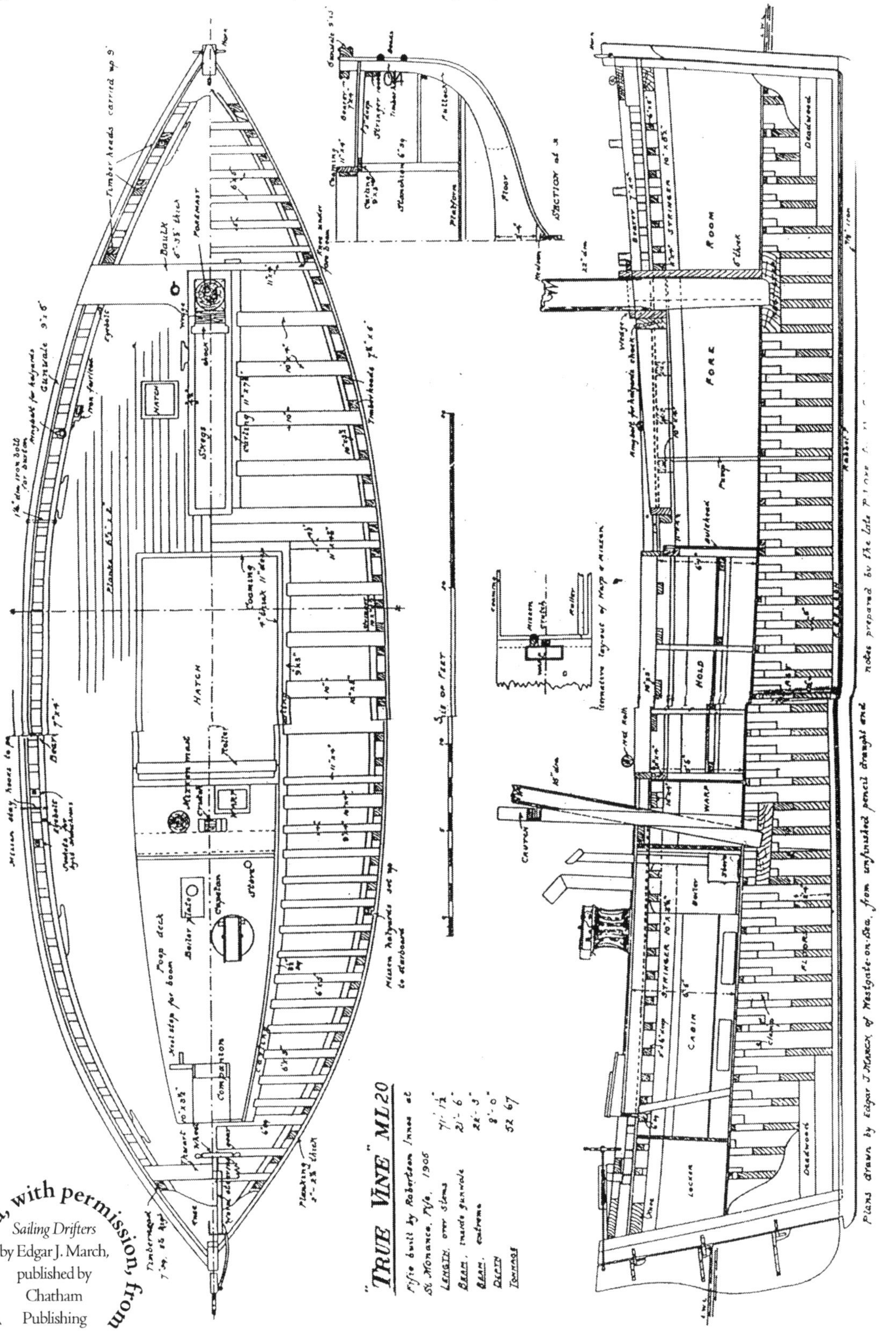

"TRUE VINE" ML20

Fifie built by Robertson Innes at
St. Monance, Fife. 1905

LENGTH. over stem		71'.1½
BEAM. inside gunwale		21'.6"
BEAM. outside		22'.3"
DEPTH		9'.0"
TONNAGE		52 67

Plans drawn by Edgar J. March of Westgate-on-Sea, from unfinished pencil draught and notes prepared by the late T. Innes (....)

Figure 15. Fifie *True Vine* ML20 (sheer, half-breadth and body plans).

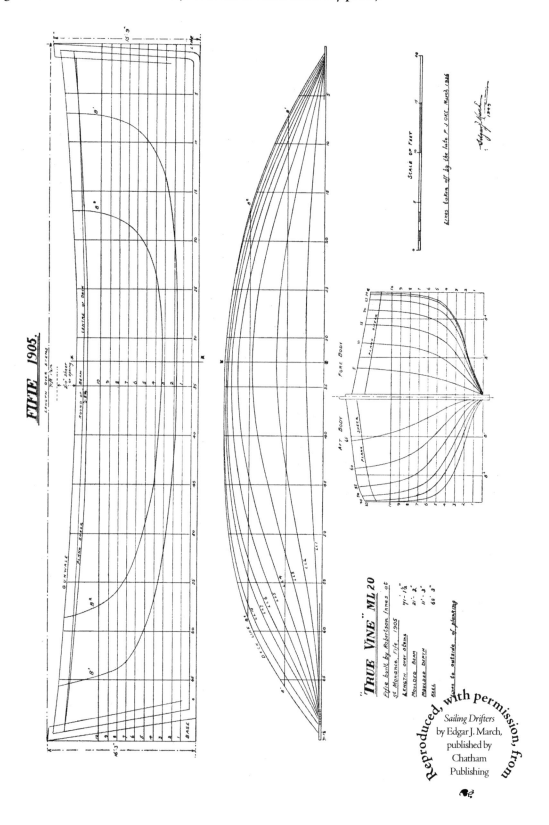

Figure 16. Fifie *True Vine* (sail plan).

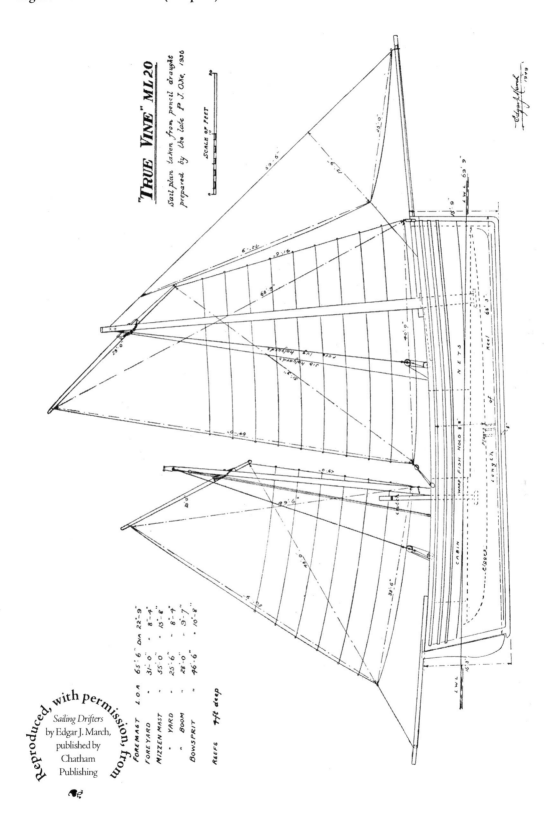

Zulu-type fishing boat, *Fidelity* **of Portessie**

At least two sets of plans are available for the big Zulu–type boats that dominated the east-coast herring fishing industry during the last years of the nineteenth century. This class of boat was characterised by a vertical stem and a deeply angled stern-post; they were, indeed, an amalgam of a Fifie and a Scaffie. As had the Fifie, the Zulu carried two dipping lug sails, the mizzen sail set to a stern-sprit with a jib sail set on a long bow sprit. Crew quarters meant that the boat could remain at sea for several weeks while the catch was taken ashore on smaller and faster schooners. The main mast was lowered onto the crutch when the boat lay to her nets and drifted with tide and wind and, where in previous years the work of lowering and raising these heavy masts had been the job of labourer crew members, the later boats were equipped with a steam capstan to ease this load on the crew.

The plans included in Figures 17 to 19 are of *Fidelity* of Portessie but other plans, even more detailed, of the Zulu *Muirneag* were drawn by a local ship surveyor and published in a set of four plans by Underhill before the boat was broken up at Stornoway in 1946.

Figure 17. Zulu *Fidelity* of Portessie (accommodation plan).

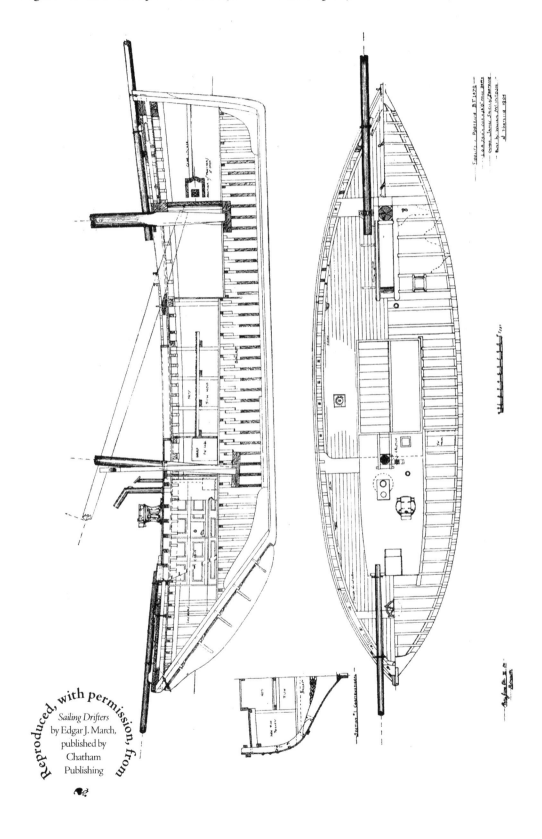

Figure 18. Zulu *Fidelity* of Portessie (sheer, half-breadth and body plans).

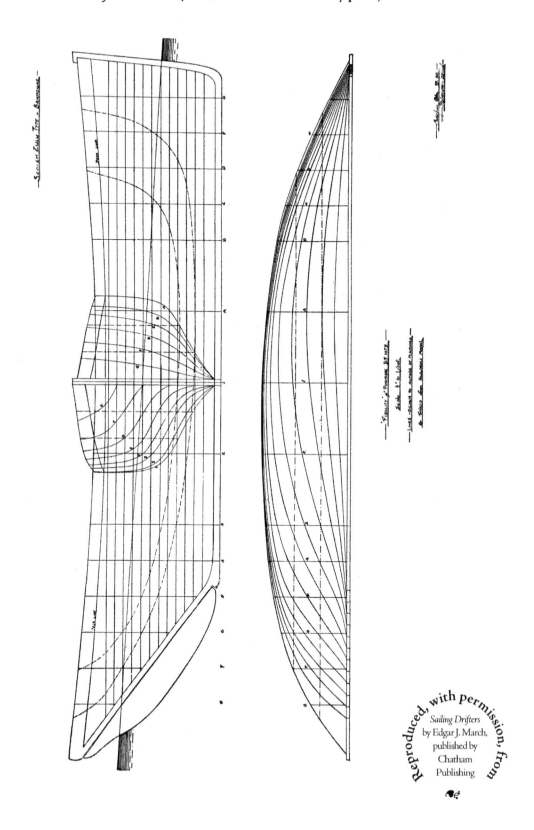

Figure 19. Zulu *Fidelity* of Portessie (sail plan).

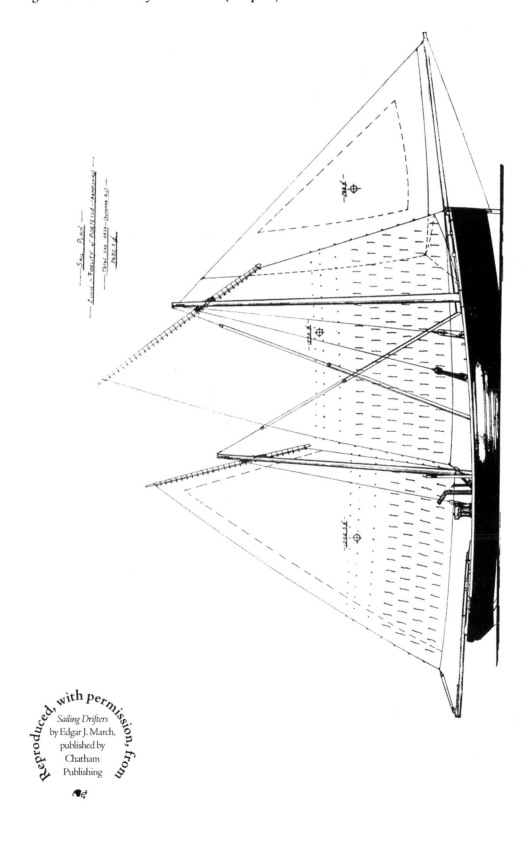

Zulu-type fishing boat, *Muirneag*

The last existing sailing drifter, *Muirneag* (SY 486), was sold at Stornoway in March 1947 for £50 to be broken up for fence posts. She had been built at Buckie in 1903 from the yard of W.R. McIntosh & Sons and had been almost continually involved in herring fishing until she was laid up at the outbreak of war in 1939. In 1946 her 80-year-old skipper, Sandy McLeod of Knock Point, Stornoway, took her to sea for the last time and in the following March she existed no more.

Fortunately, Mr. George Macleod of Stornoway took the lines off *Muirneag* and these were subsequently published in five sheets by the late Harold Underhill. Whereas the hull and general lines are little different from those of the Zulu *Fidelity*, Underhill's plans show a wealth of ornamental and constructional detail of this boat (Figures 20 to 24).

Figure 20. Zulu *Muirneag* of Stornoway (sheer, half-breadth and body plans).

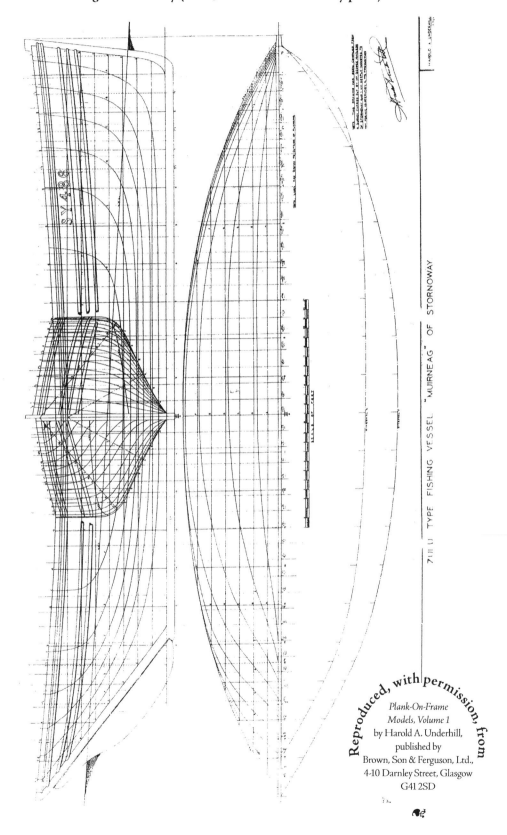

Figure 21. Zulu *Muirneag* of Stornoway (accommodation plan).

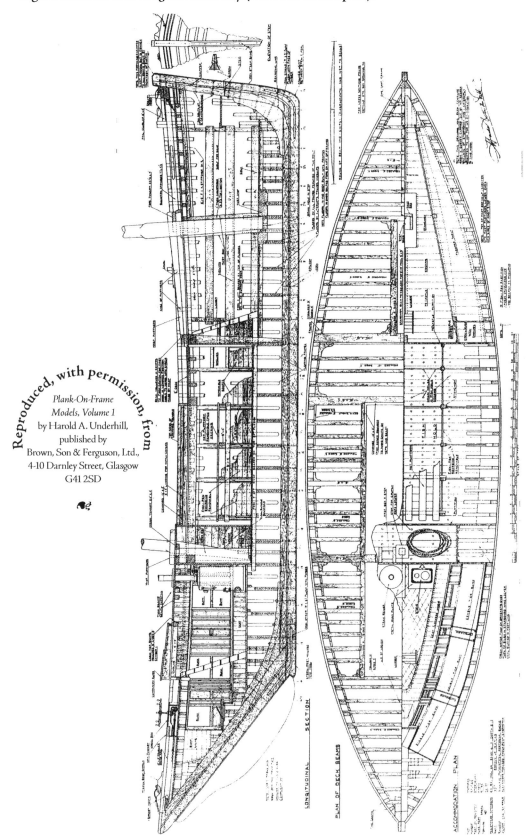

Figure 22. Zulu *Muirneag* of Stornoway (arrangement plan).

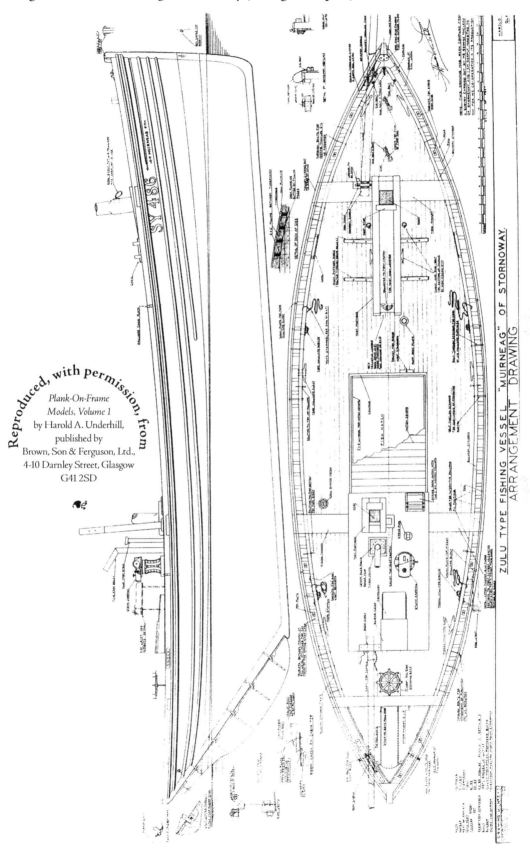

Figure 23. Zulu *Muirneag* of Stornoway (spar and rigging plans).

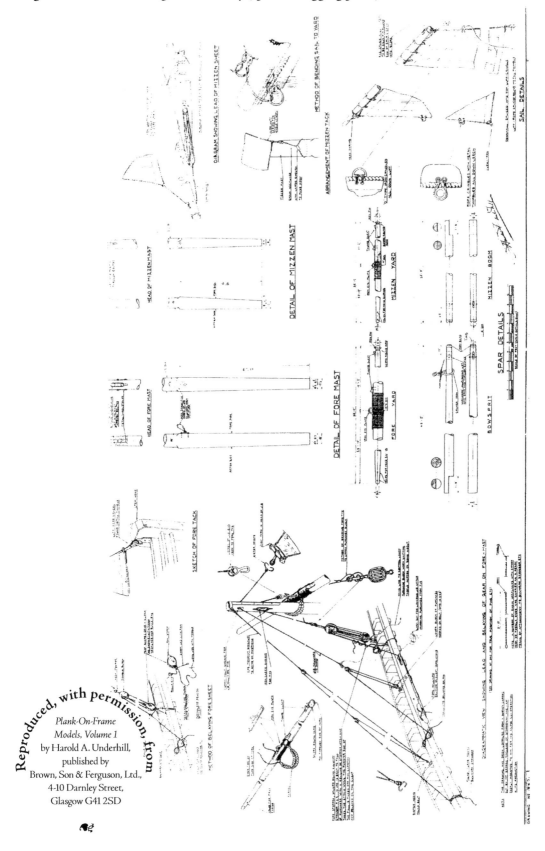

Figure 24. Zulu *Muirneag* of Stornoway (sail plan).

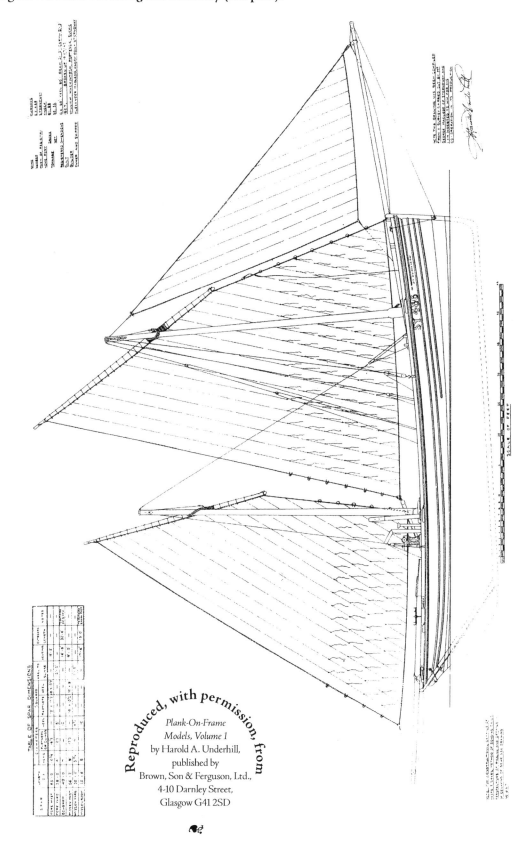

Moray Firth salmon coble

Cobles, characterised by the absence of a keel, a breadth slightly more than a third of the length and the steeply rising prow, have been in use for centuries. They were common in-shore working boats from the north-east coast of England to the Moray Firth with only minor, local, variations in design and size. The design, which allows stability in short coastal seas, good carrying capacity and the ability to cope successfully with breaking waves, probably dates from Viking times and, while for many centuries the coble was propelled by sail and oar, the boats of the middle to later twentieth century relied on outboard engines. The plans reproduced here (Figures 25 to 29) were drawn by Angus Bell and a very complete description of the construction of a coble is given by him in the journal, *Model Shipwright* (MS), No. 59 (March 1987).

The most practical difficulty in construction is the absence of a keel into which, by means of a rabbet, the garboard strakes fit closely and easily. The keel is represented by a shallow but broad beam of wood to which the two garboard strakes are applied but, in working to a miniature scale, it is difficult to make this junction accurately.

Figure 25. Moray Firth coble (lines drawing).

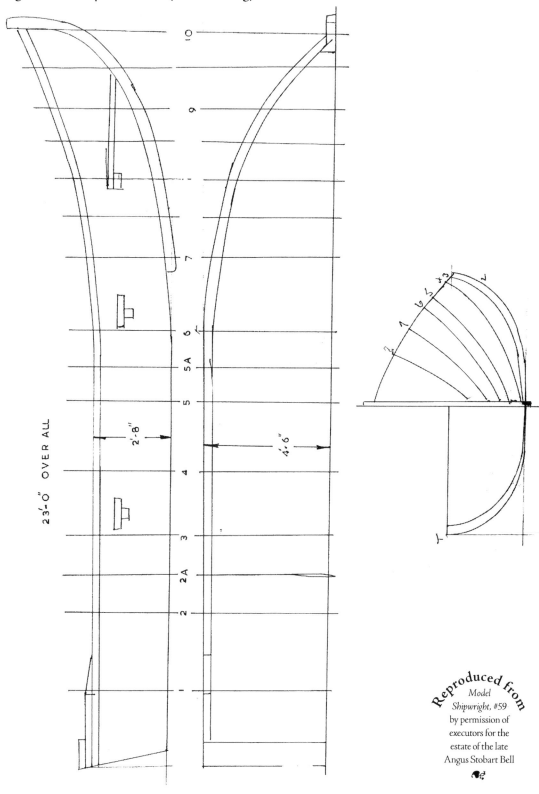

Figure 26. Moray Firth coble (constructional details 1).

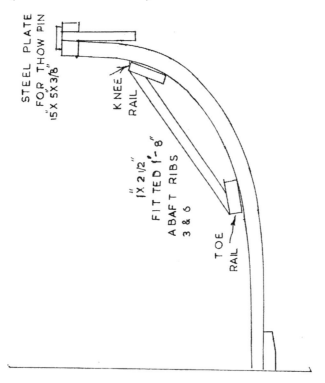

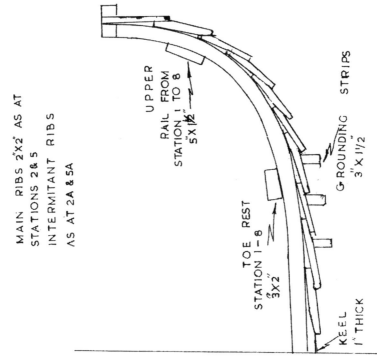

Figure 27. Moray Firth coble (constructional details 2).

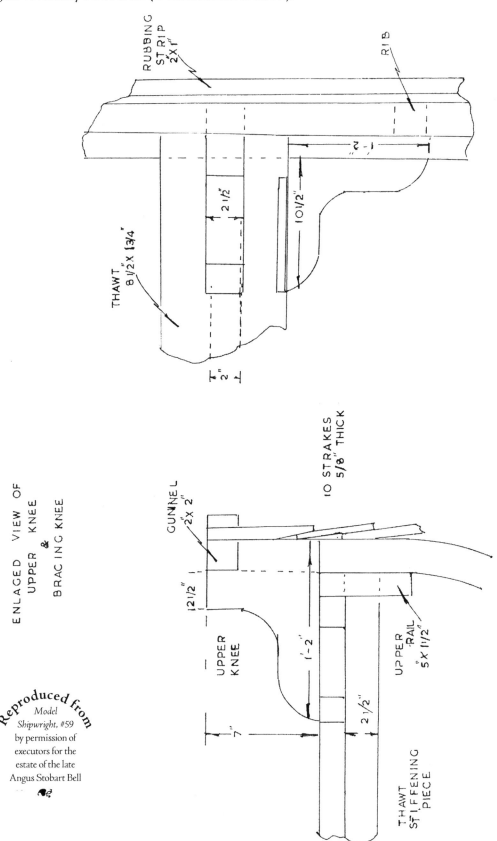

Figure 28. Moray Firth coble (constructional details 3).

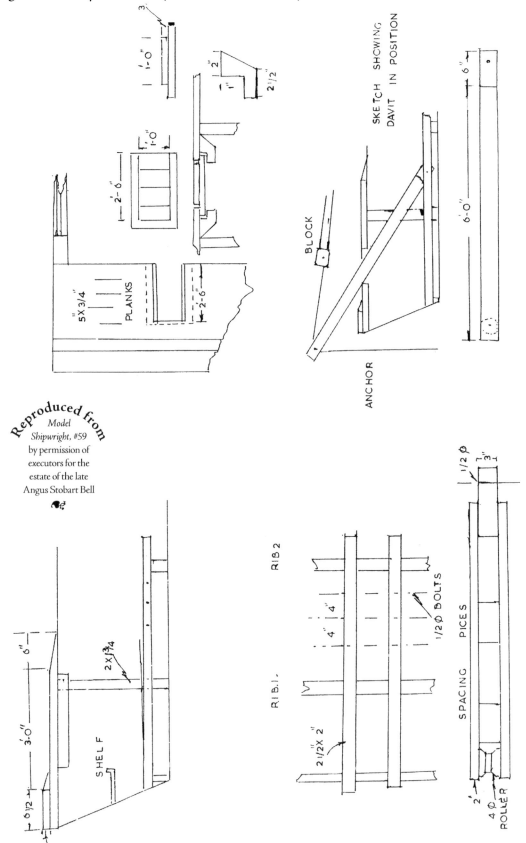

Figure 29. Moray Firth coble (constructional details 4).

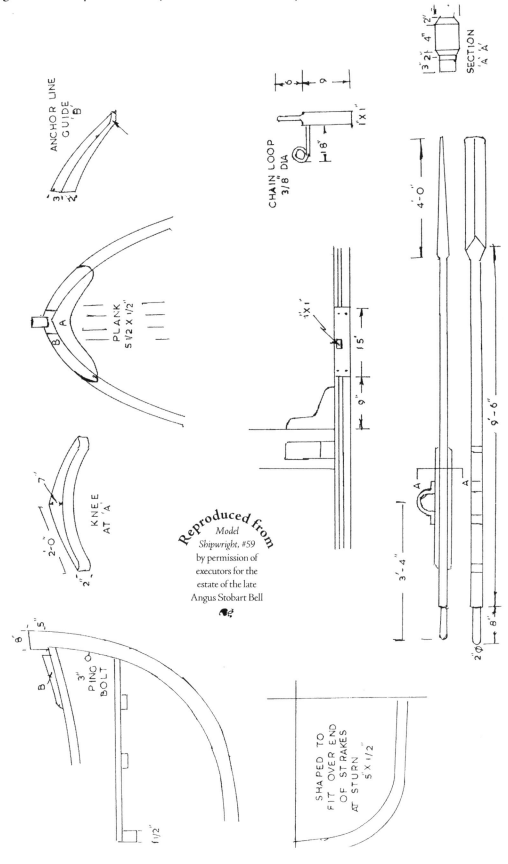

Orkney yole, *Am Bo Torraich*

Edgar March included his rather rough plans (shown in Figures 30 to 32) of a small, sixteen foot, yole from the island of Westray in a book now long out of print. The broad beam and high prow and sternpost made this boat ideal for inshore fishing in the rough waters round the Orkney islands and her overall design speaks of her Viking origins (Plates 64 and 65). The dimensions of the Westray Yole are as follows: foremast: 16 feet; foreyard: 9 feet; main mast: 14 feet; main yard: 9 feet; main boom: 9 feet; four oars: 10 feet.

The first model of this boat carried rather too much beam and because of this she was called *Am Bo Torraich* – the Pregnant Cow. The use of a Gaelic name is quite incorrect since there has never been any tradition of Gaelic speaking in the Northern Isles.

Plate 64. *Am Bo Torraich* (side).

Figure 30. Westray Yole, *Am Bo Torraich* (lines plan).

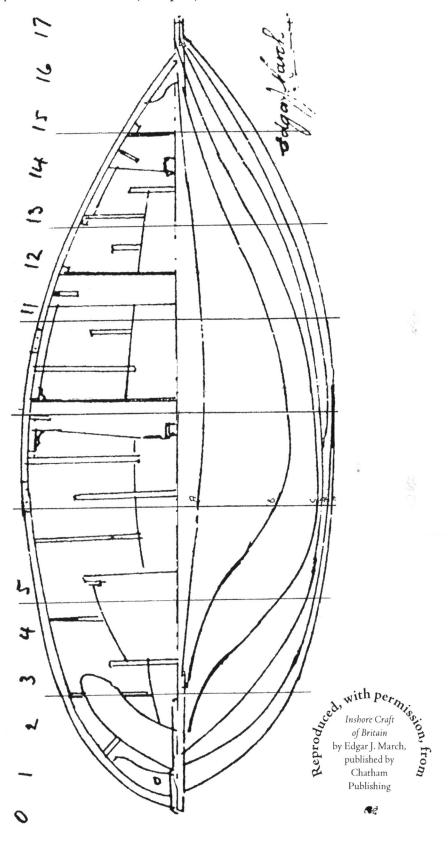

Figure 31. Westray Yole, *Am Bo Torraich* (timber details).

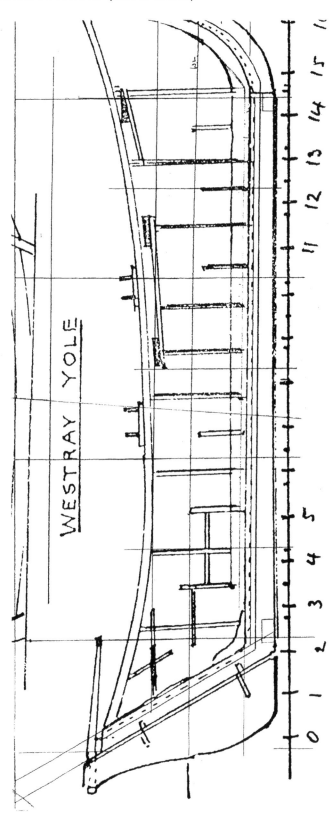

Figure 32. Westray Yole, *Am Bo Torraich* (sail plan).

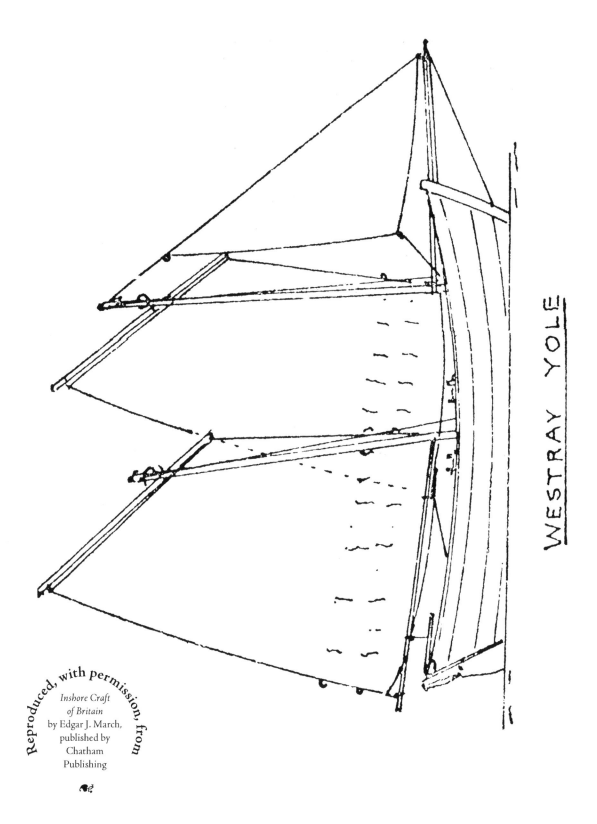

WESTRAY YOLE

Plate 65. *Am Bo Torraich* (top).

Shetland's first engine-powered fishing boat, *Owner's Delight*

The following are believed to be the only plans in existence of *Owner's Delight*, the 37 foot haddock boat built in 1911 by Thos. Walter Scott of Scalloway, Shetland, for Mr. William Goodlad of Burra Isle. I first heard of her in 1988 through the reader's-letters pages of a copy of *Yachting World* (Figure 33) and, after contacting the writer to *Yachting World*, I was sent plans of her new accommodation when the boat was converted from a commercial craft to a sailing yacht in 1937. A Mr. Moncrieff of Lerwick had been responsible for that conversion and from him I received a photograph of *Owner's Delight* at her launch in 1911 (Figure 34) and a note that she had had several names: *Owner's Delight, Hawk, Renown* and finally *Veng*. The conversion from a commercial boat to a yacht would have left the essential hull lines and construction unaltered while the photograph of her on her launch date gave some idea of her deck layout and there was thus sufficient information available to build a realistic model (Figures 35 & 36; Plate 66).

In 1911 *Owner's Delight* was originally fitted with a Bolsover steam engine but as this proved to be unreliable and under-powered, the engine was replaced with an Alpha hot-bulb and, finally, with a Kelvin petrol-paraffin engine. Steering was by wheel with a worm-drive system to the rudder and she was clinker built over heavy frames.

The dimensions of spars are:main mast: 14 feet; main gaff: 8 feet; mizzen mast: 8½ feet; mizzen boom: 5 feet.

Figure 33. The letter that started the search for plans of *Owner's Delight.*

Well travelled Veng

Sir, We are currently researching the history of the old Shetland cutter *Veng* which we owned from 1976 to 1980 and wonder if any of your readers could help.

Veng was built by Thomas Walter Scott of Scalloway and launched in 1911. She is a 37ft (11·3m) double-ender, of clinker construction, in the style of a Shetland six-areen, originally called *Owner's Delight.* We know a good deal of her early history from Tom Moncrieff of Lerwick, who renamed her *Veng* and converted her to a Bermudan ketch just before the war (although by the time we acquired her she had been re-rigged as a cutter).

We have, so far, discovered very little about her travels in the post-war period from 1945 to 1976. We believe she may have been as far as the Danube, and traces of toredo worm also bear witness to a spell in warmer waters.

GAVIN AND GEORGIE McLAREN,
Plockton, Ross-shire

Figure 34. *Owner's Delight* **on her launch date.**

Newly launched from Hay & Company's yard at Blacksness, Scalloway in 1911, is the clinker-built vessel "Owner's Delight", built for Robert Goodlad of Hamnavoe for haddock line fishing. She was 34½ ft long overall and in addition to sails she had an auxiliary steam engine – hence her claim to be the first steamer built in Shetland.
In later changes of ownership she became the "Hawk", "Brown" and "Veng". Under the latter name she is still doing service as a pleasure craft based on the Firth of Clyde.

(Photo Alwyn Anderson collection)

Figure 35. *Owner's Delight* (lines plan).

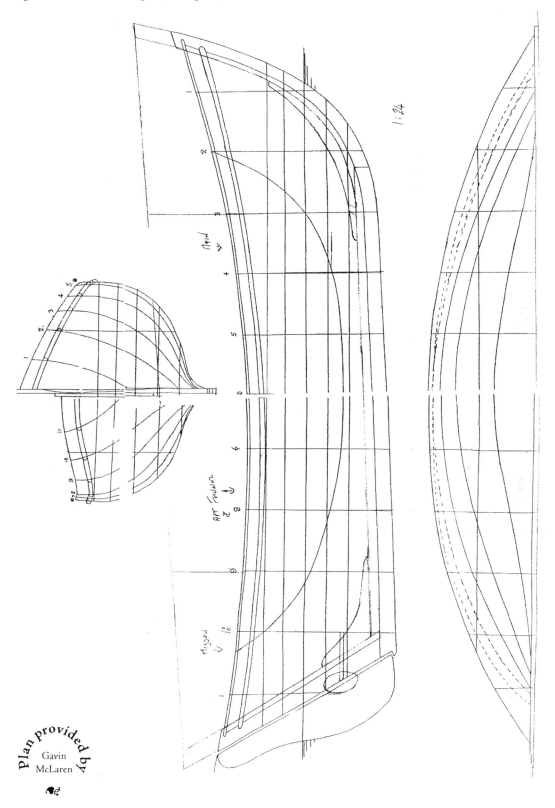

Figure 36. *Owner's Delight,* 1937 conversion (accommodation plan).

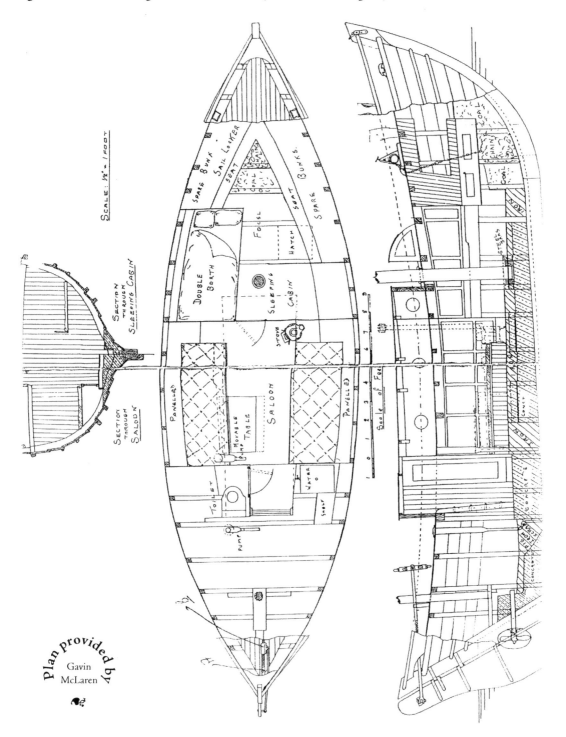

Plate 66. *Owner's Delight,* scale 1:12.

A Shetland Sixareen, *Water Witch*

When one looks at Figure 37, Viking heritage of the sixareen is immediately obvious and these light, clinker-built craft were intended to be rowed, by a double bank of six oars, when there was a lack of wind, and to be hauled up a beach beyond the high-water mark. The single mast was stepped almost amidships and stayed with shrouds, there being no reinforced mast trunk as in many East-coast boats. The sail was held by a short forestay to a hole through the stemhead while the main sheet passed through a hole in the gunwale, back through a cringle in the clew of the sail, and was then held by the helmsman. There were usually five or six removable thwarts, or tafts, and close to the helmsman's thwart was a hand operated bilge pump although there was also a deep wooden shovel for bailing.

Sixareens were built for deep-water line fishing for cod and ling and, if the weather allowed, the boats could stay at sea in Spring and Summer for several days. Lines carrying up to 1,200 hooks would be set and the maximum catch that a Sixareen could carry was about 1½ tons. As it was an open boat, the risk of foundering by being swamped by a sudden wave was ever present.

Shetland Foureen or Yole

The little sister of the Sixareen was the Foureen (shown in Figure 38), propelled by a very similar sail on a central mast, or by a bank of four oars. The Foureen was normally used for inshore line fishing as a day boat, or for crab and lobster fishing.

Figure 37. Shetland Sixareen, *Water Witch*.

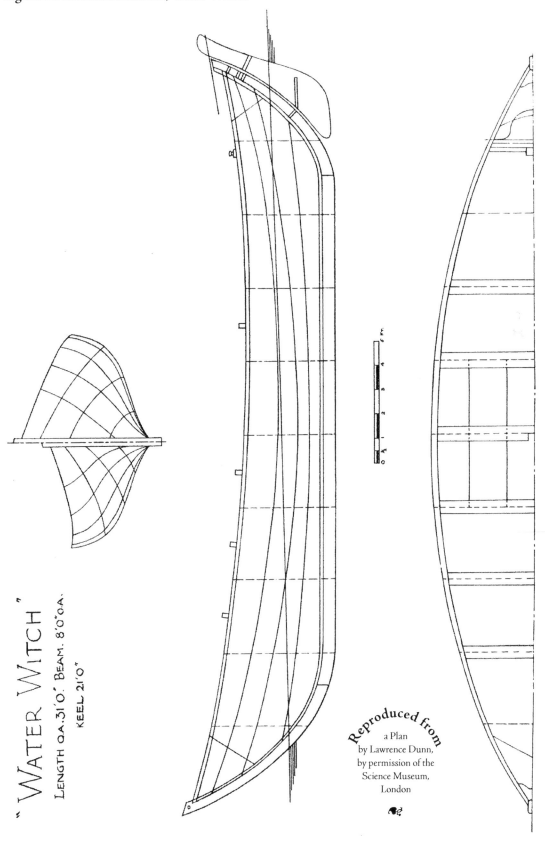

"WATER WITCH"
LENGTH O.A. 31' 0". BEAM. 8' 0" O.A.
KEEL 21' 0"

Reproduced from
a Plan
by Lawrence Dunn,
by permission of the
Science Museum,
London

Figure 38. Shetland Foureen.

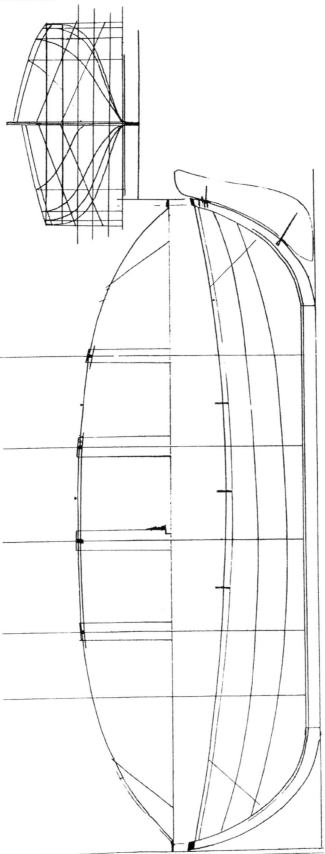

West-coast boats

There was in general a greater variation in the design, size and style of West-Coast boats than there was on the East Coast, principally because of three factors. Prior to the latter third of the nineteenth century, most boats fished in sheltered sea lochs, road and rail links to southern markets were few or non-existent and a commercial fishery was thus less viable. Additionally, regular visits to sea lochs by the herring shoals were much less predictable than in the North Sea. Much of the fishing was thus line or creel fishing and deep-sea herring fishing was virtually confined to East-Coast boats, of Fifie and Zulu design, that fished in the Minch or to the west of the Outer Hebrides and returned with their catch to East-Coast ports such as Aberdeen and Buckie.

Ness skiff, *An Sgoth Niseach*

This very distinctive design (shown in figures 39 to 41) was confined to the northern Lewis port of Ness and was used for cod and ling fishing during the last quarter of the nineteenth century. Boats were characteristically double enders, with a keel length of 21 feet and an overall length of 30 to 32 feet. The origin of her distinctive 'gun-port' markings on the uppermost strake is thought to have been influenced by the appearance of men-of-war in the nineteenth century.

The only remaining skiff was built in 1935 and has a 15-foot keel but in 1994 a local shipwright, John Murdo MacLeod, built a full-size version of the *Sgoth* (her construction was featured in a BBC television programme). An excellent account of the construction of a model of the smaller *Sgoth* can be found in *Model Shipwright* 99 (March 1997) by her builder, Rev. Donald MacQuarrie (Plate 67).

Figure 39. *An Sgoth Niseach* (lines plan).

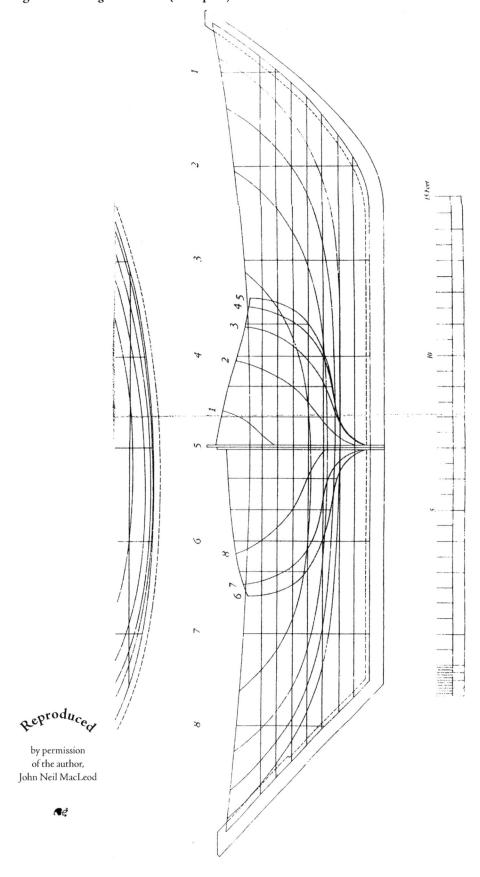

Figure 40. *An Sgoth Niseach* (hull plan).

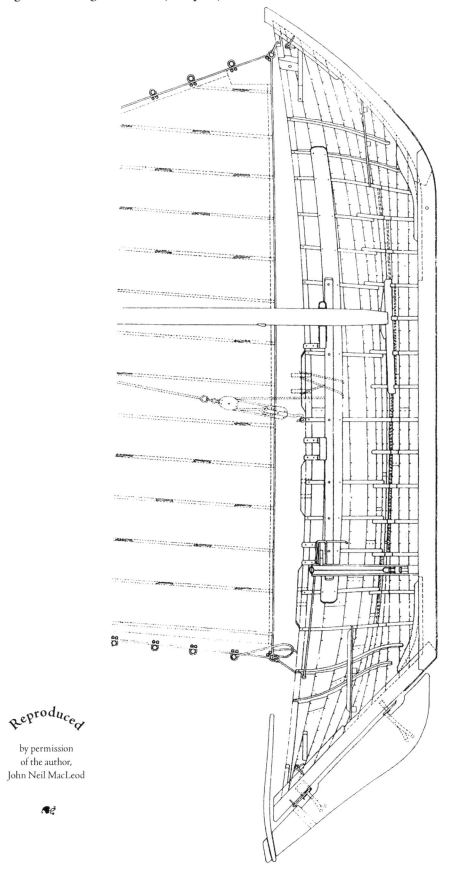

Figure 41. *An Sgoth Niseach* (half-breadth plan).

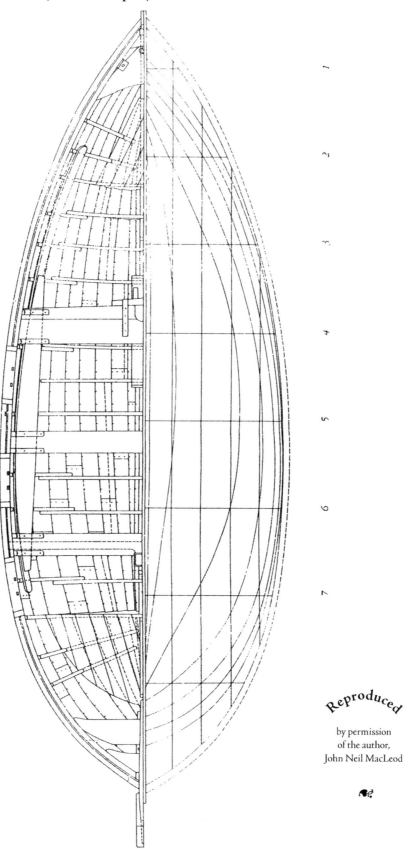

Plate 67. *An Sgoth Niseach.*

Ness Yole

> The similarity of this small 14-foot craft (shown in Figure 42) to the Shetland Foureen is obvious and points to a shared ancestry with Viking boats. The *Ness Yole* was used for inshore line-and-creel fishing, for personal and family use rather than for any commercial fishing.

The Grimsay double-ender

> This elegant double gaff rigged fishing boat originated in the early 1880's and probably had its roots in the small work boats common along the western coasts of Scotland and Ireland. The Grimsay boats of North Uist were principally used for lobster fishing and when engine power began to replace sails, the relatively straight stern of the Grimsay boats allowed this conversion to be made with little difficulty.
>
> The plans of this boat (shown in Figures 43 & 44) and the information about her were kindly given by Rev. Donald MacQuarrie, who also built the model illustrated in Plate 68. The boat, 'Welcome Home' C.Y. 275, was built in 1933 by Charles Stewart for Neil MacInnes and had a length of 26 feet and a breadth of 8 feet.

Figure 42. *Ness Yole.*

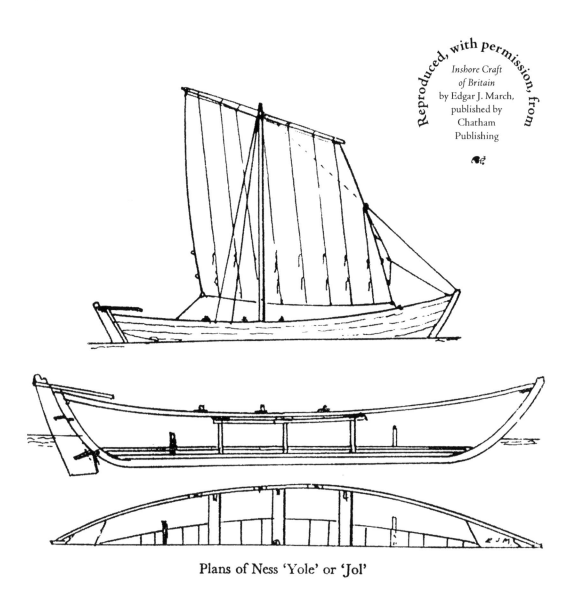

Plans of Ness 'Yole' or 'Jol'

Figure 43. Grimsay double-ender, *Welcome Home* (lines plan)

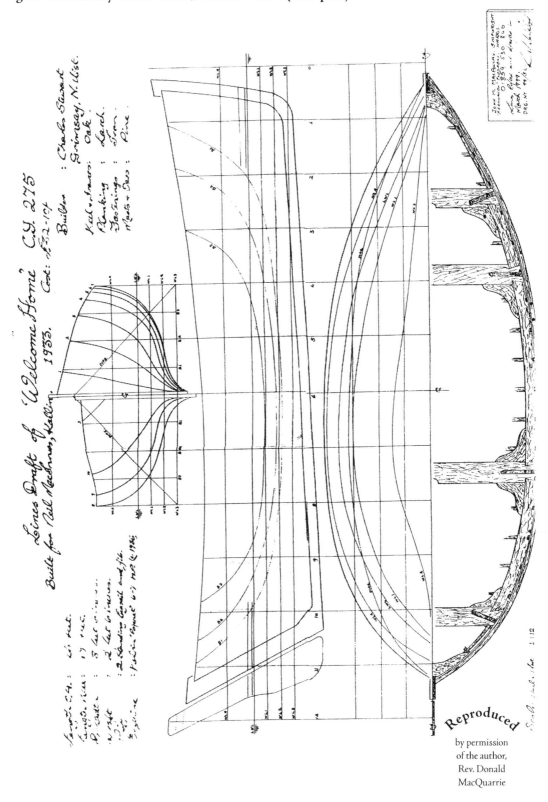

Figure 44. Grimsay double-ender, *Welcome Home* **(sail plan)**

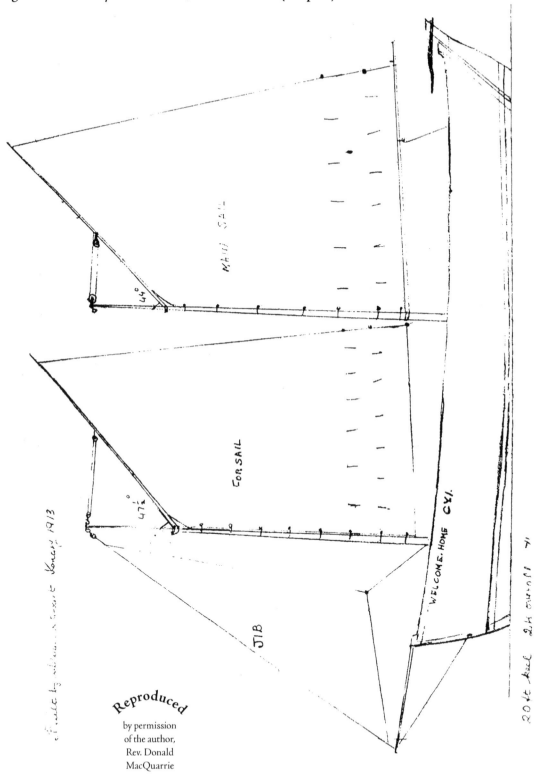

Plate 68. Grimsay double-ender, *Welcome Home.*

Fifie skiff, *Bounty* (UL 217)

This little skiff (shown in Plates 69 & 70), with a keel length of only 22 feet, is of Fifie design, and was registered in Ullapool. She was used for herring fishing in the west-coast sea-lochs close to Loch Broom and probably further afield. As with many inshore boats of her date and design, she was an open clench-built boat powered by a single dipping-lug sail and four 14-foot oars.

The dimensions of *Bounty* were: length overall: 24 feet; beam: 8 feet, 6 inches; depth 3 feet; mast: 22 feet, 6 to 4 inches diameter; yard: 17 feet; four oars: 14 feet (Figure 45).

Plate 69. Fifie skiff, *Bounty*, UL 217.

Plate 70. Fifie skiff, *Bounty*, UL 217 (top view).

Figure 45. *Bounty,* **UL 217 (plans).**

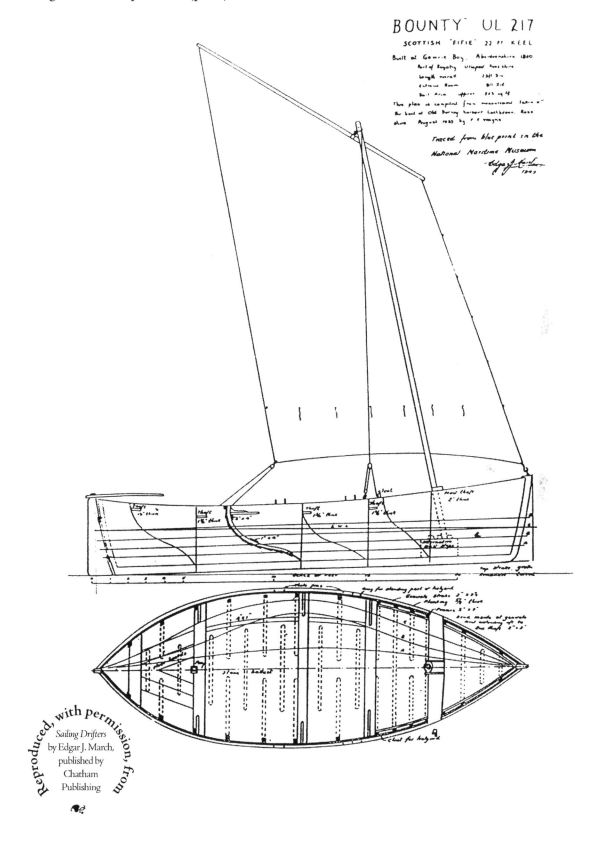

Duncan the Post's boat

During the early 1980s an article appeared in the *Scotsman* newspaper regarding the finding in a crofter's field of an old, and small, lug-sailed boat that had been used by the Ullapool postman to deliver mail across Loch Broom in the early years of the twentieth century. The remains of the boat were taken to Leicester by Mr Bill Bailiff, the original owner of a firm called Character Boats and he kindly provided a set of plans for the boat (Figure 46). A detailed description of building a model of *Duncan the Post's* boat appears in the magazine, *Model Shipwright* 73 (September 1990). The resulting model is pictured in Plates 71 to 75. While delivering the mail was perhaps the *raison d'être* of the boat it would have been typical of crofters' boats of the period and as such would also have been used for fishing.

Plate 71. *Duncan the Post's* boat (side).

Figure 46. Ullapool Post boat (plans).

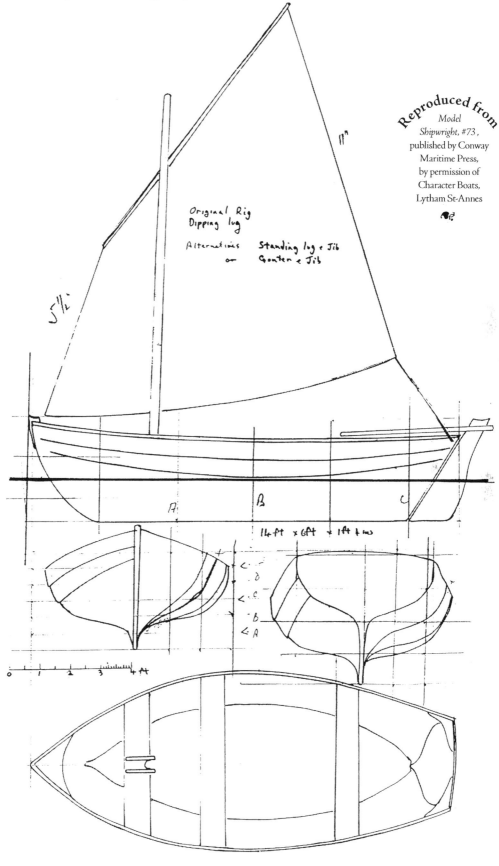

Plate 72. *Duncan the Post's* boat (top).

Plate 73. Duncan at the helm.

Plate 74. *Duncan the Post's* boat (interior view).

Plate 75. *Duncan the Post's* boat (interior of stern section).

Oban skiff, *Gylen*

This delightful, small, clench-built boat (shown in Plates 76 & 77) dates from about 1880 and her full and rounded stern was typical of boat design in the Oban area. She was used for line fishing or for crab and lobster, and would have seldom ventured further afield than the sea areas west of Oban and north-west towards the Sound of Mull. She takes her name from the ruined castle at the south end of the island of Kerrera.

The dimensions of the Oban Skiff were: length overall: 23 feet, 6 inches; depth: 2 feet, 3 inches; mast: 19 feet, 4 to 3 inches diameter; yard: 13 feet; bowsprit: 6 feet (2 feet inboard; two or four oars: 8 feet (Figures 47 & 48).

Plate 76. Oban skiff, *Gylen* (side).

Plate 77. Oban skiff, *Gylen* (top).

Figure 47. Oban skiff (plans).

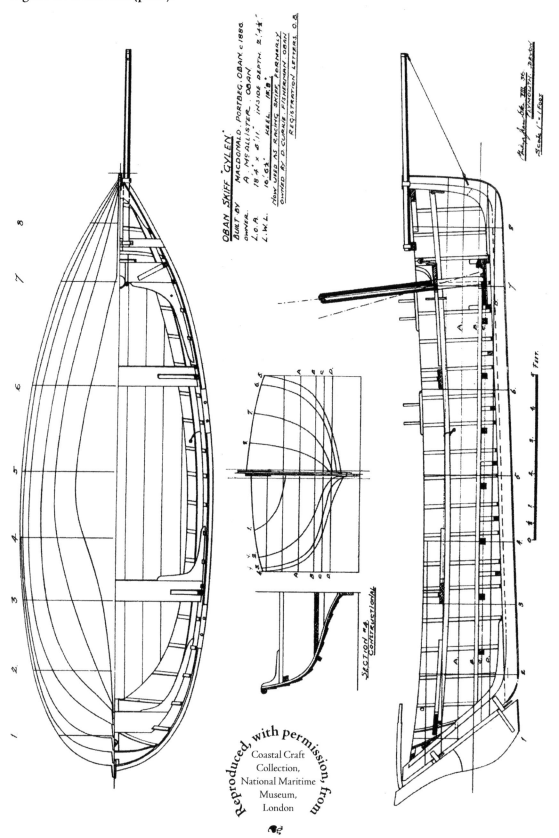

Figure 48. Oban skiff (sail plan).

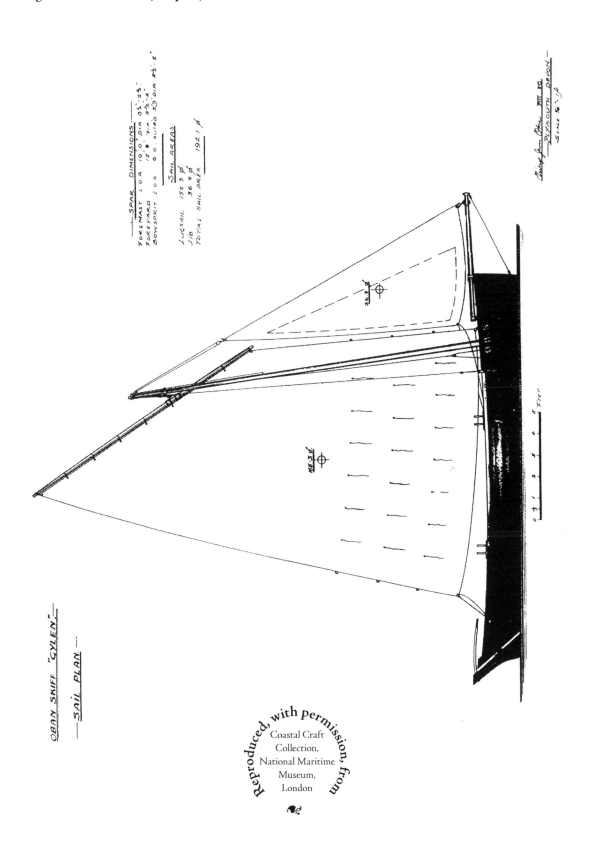

Loch Fyne skiff, *Bonny Jean* (TT 177)

Bonnie Jean (Plates 78 & 79), a part-decked Zulu skiff was built in about 1870 by Henderson of Tarbert for a Robert Bruce of Ardrishaig, and is a good example of a half-decked boat. She measured 35 feet overall by just over 11 feet in width and had a depth of 6 feet, 3 inches. The fore deck measured 13 feet, 6 inches and the cabin below this deck had a coal burning stove, two fixed bunks, some storage space, a chain locker and two hammock-type bunks.

Aft of the fore cabin were two net platforms set a foot or so below the gunwale. The 35-foot mast was stepped in a strong trunk of 5 feet, 8 inches and the bowsprit measured 13 feet, 6 inches overall, of which 9 feet, 6 inches was outboard. The boat carried a triangular foresail and a dipping lug as the main and had a bilge pump set into the sternmost thwart. *Bonnie Jean* generally fished within the relatively sheltered waters of Loch Fyne and the southernmost stretches of the Clyde estuary, although she may have travelled to the outer Hebrides by way of the Crinan Canal. She carried four oars, each 20 feet in length. Plans for Bonnie Jean are provided in Figure 49.

Plate 78. Zulu skiff, *Bonnie Jean* (side).

Plate 79. Zulu skiff, *Bonnie Jean* (top).

Figure 49. *Bonnie Jean* (plans).

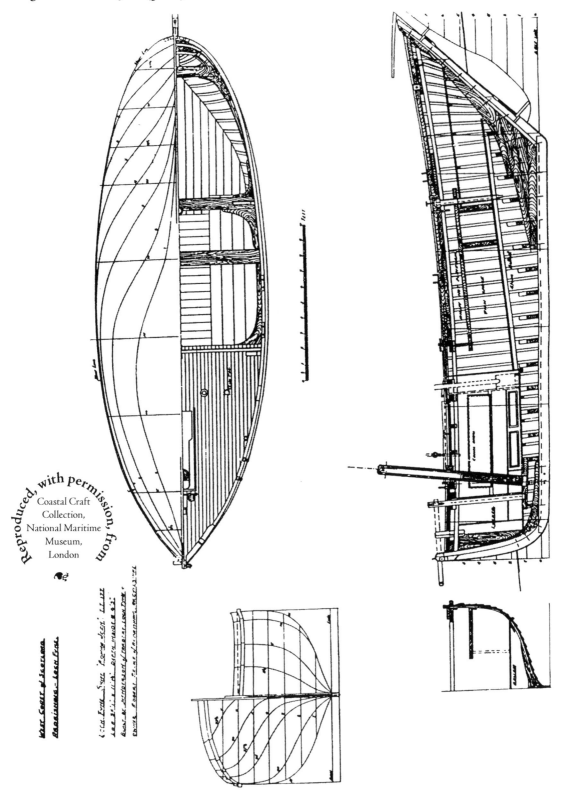

Zulu skiff, *Snowdrop* of Ardrishaig

Snowdrop (Plates 80 & 81), a fully open boat of 22 feet, 6 inches in length, was built in 1907 by Archibald Munro of Ardrishaig for skipper Dan McLachlan. With a width of 6 feet, 6 inches she carried a single dipping-lug sail on a single mast set at a raking angle about 2 feet from the bow (Figures 50 & 51). As a fully open boat she was more at risk to being pooped by a heavy or following sea and it is thus probable that she confined her fishing to the relatively sheltered waters in or south of Loch Fyne.

Plate 80. Zulu skiff, *Snowdrop* of Ardrishaig.

Plate 81. Zulu skiff, *Snowdrop* of Ardrishaig (interior).

Figure 50. Zulu skiff, *Snowdrop* of Ardrishaig (plans)

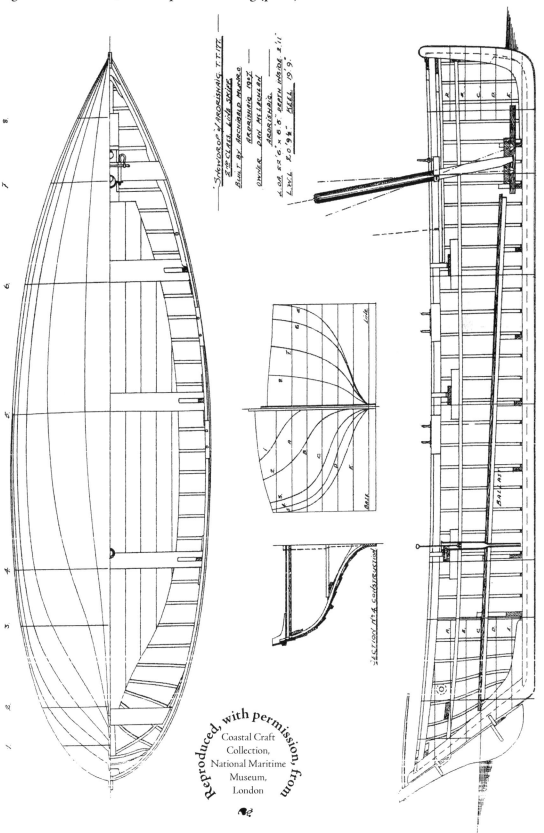

Figure 51. Zulu skiff, *Snowdrop* of Ardrishaig (sail plan)

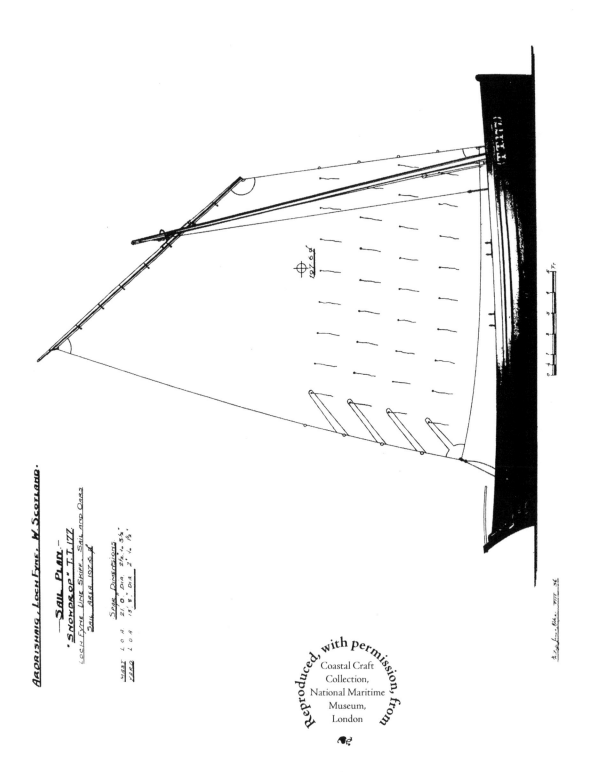

Fifie line skiff

This delightfully delicate-seeming skiff was built at Fairlie by the firm of Boag in about 1890 and was used, as her description states, for line rather than for net fishing. Although Oke's plans of the boat state that she was a 'Largs line skiff', she was owned by Robert Bruce of Ardrishaig, at the mouth of Loch Fyne and presumably fished in Loch Fyne and the more open waters of the mouth of the Clyde estuary.

Figure 52 shows the detail necessary to build an accurate model of the boat while the sail arrangements are shown in Figure 53. The spar lengths are: mast: 18 feet; lug-yard: 11 feet, 3 inches; and the sprit: 7 feet, 5 inches. The sail plan was a dipping lug of 125 square feet with a short jib of 27½ square feet. Her crew would normally consist of two men or the skipper and a boy, and two sets of 12-foot oars would be used in the absence of wind.

Figure 52. Largs line skiff (plans).

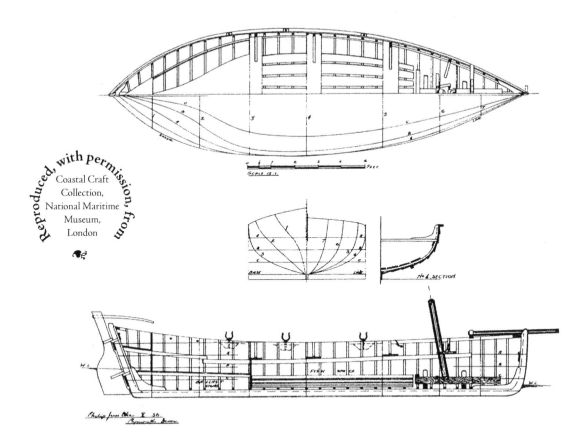

Figure 53. Largs line skiff (sail plan).

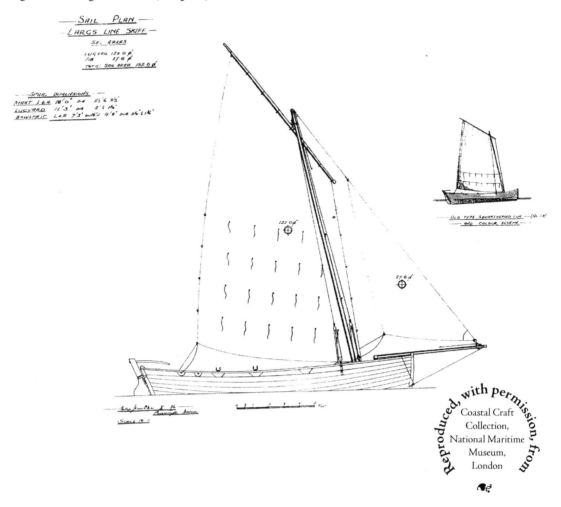

Loch Fyne Zulu skiff, *Aye Ready*

The origins of the rather brief plans of this boat are unknown but, as she is clearly a fully decked boat, it is probable that she was built during the last two decades of the nineteenth century. The plans (Figure 54) show a wide fish hatch that would have been closed and thus made relatively water tight with wooden battens; a steering hatch or rather a steering well in the stern; and a longer narrower hatch in the bow that would have held the mast trunk and the wooden wedges to ensure that the mast rake was at the angle that the skipper required.

Aye Ready was designed and built by D. Munro & Son of Blairmore, in north-west Sutherland, and was 42 feet long overall with a maximum breadth of 12 feet.

Figure 54. Zulu skiff, *Aye Ready* (plans).

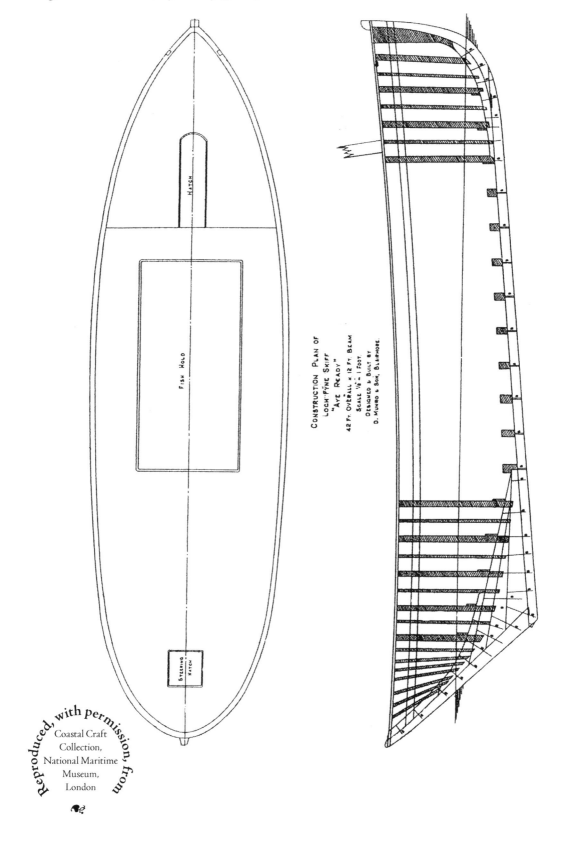

CONSTRUCTION PLAN OF
LOCH-FYNE SKIFF
"AYE READY"
42 FT. OVERALL × 12 FT. BEAM
SCALE ½" = 1 FOOT.
DESIGNED & BUILT BY
D. MUNRO & SON, BLAIRMORE.

FISH HOLD

HATCH

STEERING HATCH

Zulu skiff, *Jean Morgan*

This little Zulu skiff (shown in Plates 82 & 83) was originally called *Maggie Campbell of Girvan* but when her lines were drawn by Philip Oke in the 1930s (Figure 55), she was owned by a Mr. Hunter of Portpatrick. She was built in about 1890 and originated in a yard in Girvan.

Her length overall was 22 feet, 10 inches with a beam of 6 feet, 11 inches and a keel length of 19 feet, 10inches. She carried a dipping-lug main sail and a jib-sail carried on a bowsprit. As with many other boats of this size she was a line fisher and would normally carry a crew of two or three, with a very local fishing beat close inshore. In the absence of wind progress homewards would have been with four oars each of about 12 feet in length.

Plate 82. Zulu skiff, *Jean Morgan*.

Plate 83. Zulu skiff, *Jean Morgan* (interior).

Figure 55. Zulu skiff, *Jean Morgan* (plans).

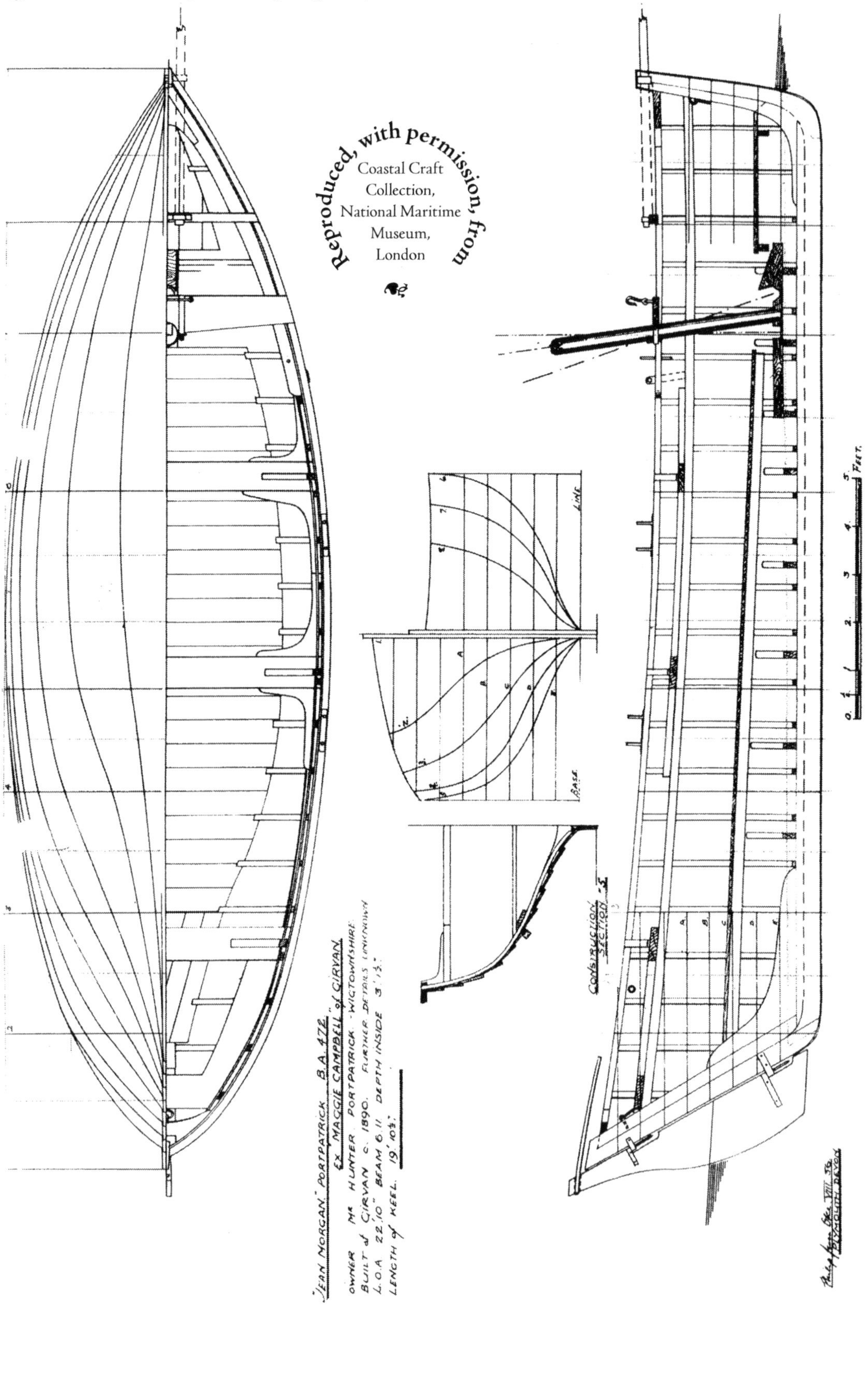

Portpatrick line skiff, *Brothers*

The skiff shown in Plates 84 to 86 is one of the most enjoyable boats to build (see plans shown in Figures 56 & 57). She was a 'busy little boat', only just over 19 feet in length and 6 feet, 8 inches in breadth but with a main and a fore mast and five thwarts. When loaded with oars, sails and all the other equipment carried by such a boat, it is incredible that there was still room for a catch of fish.

Brothers was built in 1898 by a Mr. McDowall for a Thomas Muir of Portpatrick and she was registered at Ballantrae, with her number being B.A. 318. The Scottish Fisheries Museum in Anstruther has a transcript of a tape-recorded conversation with one of the daughters of the two brothers who owned the boat, describing her involvement when her uncle ended a day's fishing.

Plate 84. Portpatrick line skiff, *Brothers*.

Plate 85. Portpatrick line skiff, *Brothers* (interior).

Plate 86. Portpatrick line skiff, *Brothers* (top).

Figure 56. Portpatrick line skiff, *Brothers* **(lines plan).**

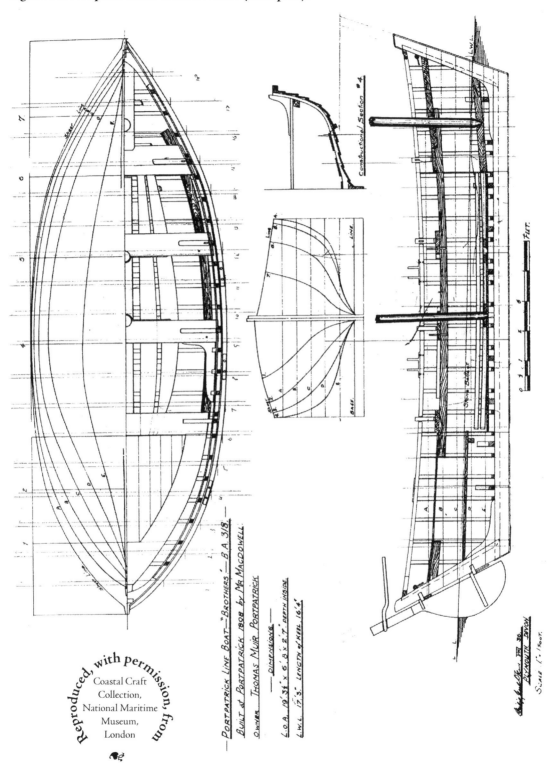

— PORTPATRICK LINE BOAT—"BROTHERS'—B.A. 3/8 —

BUILT at PORTPATRICK 1898 by MR MACDOWELL

OWNER THOMAS MUIR PORTPATRICK.

— DIMENSIONS.—

L.O.A 19'3½' × 6'A × 2'7'. DEPTH INSIDE

L.W.L. 17'3". LENGTH O/ KEIL 16'4'.

Figure 57. Portpatrick line skiff, *Brothers* (sail plan).

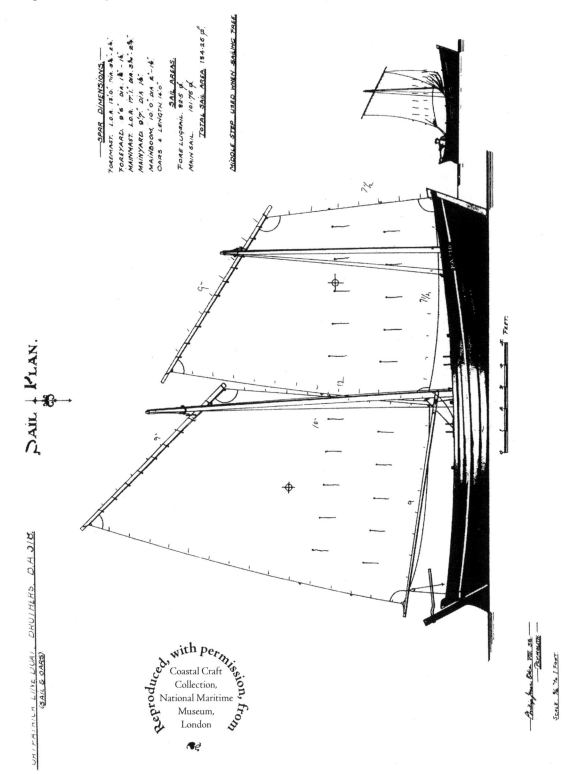

Solway Firth net whammel, *Dora*

This little boat, only 19 feet, 3 inches in length, is a very interesting craft, as can be seen in Plates 87 & 88. She was built by James Wilson of Annan, Waterfoot in 1900 and was previously owned by a John Robinson of Annan. At that time there was a fleet of 30 to 40 salmon whammels built and working from Annan, which surprisingly has no harbour. Whammels used a trawl net to catch salmon and were fitted with two water-tight compartments midships to act as buoyancy aids in the often rough and turbulent waters of the Solway Firth. Plans for *Dora* are shown in Figures 58 & 59.

Plate 87. Solway Firth net whammel, *Dora* (side).

Plate 88. Solway Firth net whammel, *Dora* (top).

Figure 58. Solway Firth net whammel, *Dora* (lines plan).

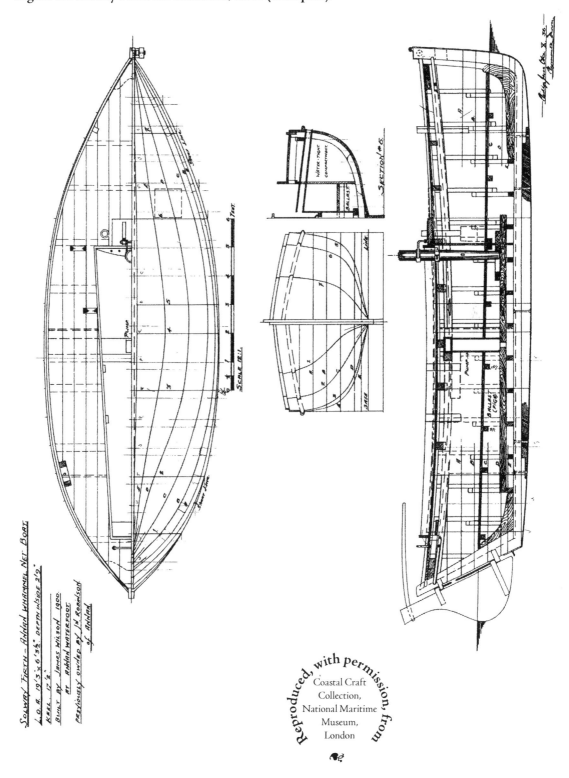

Figure 59. Solway Firth net whammel, *Dora* (sail plan).

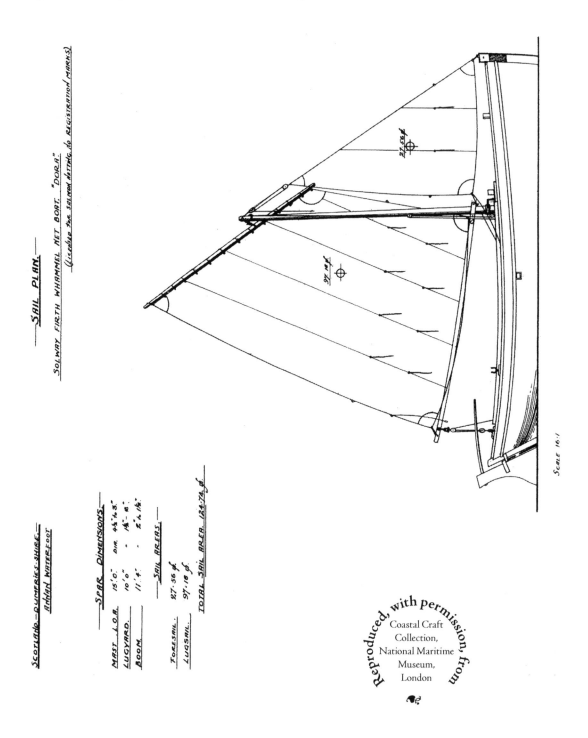

SAIL PLAN.

SOLWAY FIRTH WHAMMEL NET BOAT. "DORA."

(Lineslip the salvon netting. No registration marks)

27.56 gf

97 14 gf

SCALE 16:1

SCOTLAND.—DUMFRIES-SHIRE.
Annan Waterfoot

SPAR DIMENSIONS.

MAST J.O.B.	15.0"	DIA. 4½"×3"
LUGYARD.	10'0"	" 1½"-1½"
BOOM.	11'4"	" 2"×1½"

SAIL AREAS.

FORESAIL. 27.56 gf
LUGSAIL. 97.18 gf

TOTAL SAIL AREA. 124.74 gf

Location of models

To date (March 2005) a total of 25 models that I have built, not all different, are in public museums, with about the same number in the homes of family and friends. The locations of models on indefinite loan to museums are as follows.

The Scottish Fisheries Museum Trust, Anstruther

The collection of models are all at a scale of 1:12, and this has been a positive intent, so that the different sizes and methods of construction of each boat can be appreciated and compared. This collection at present includes:

1845 Newhaven Fifie, *Silver Harvest*

Loch Fyne skiff, *Snowdrop*

Largs skiff, *Jean Morgan*

Solway Firth whammel, *Dora*

Orkney Yole

Oban skiff, *Gylen*

Moray Firth Scaffie, *Gratitude*

Loch Fyne skiff, *Bonnie Jean*

Portpatrick skiff, *Brothers*

Ullapool Fifie, *Bounty*

Shetland boat, *Owner's Delight*

1845 Buckie Scaffie, *Aye Hameward*

Nairn Fishertown Museum

The five models in this collection are all at a scale of 1:24, again to allow comparison between different boats designed to work in different sea conditions. This collection includes:

North Sea Fifie (74 feet overall)

Moray Firth Scaffie, *Gratitude*

1845 Moray Firth Scaffie

Ullapool skiff, *Bounty*

1845 Newhaven Fifie

Helmsdale Heritage Museum.

Small, 36-foot, east coast Fifie, *John Morton II* at 1:12 scale.

Ullapool Museum

Fifie skiff, *Bounty* at 1:12 scale.

Annan museum (all at 1:12 scale)

Solway Firth net whammel, *Dora*

Solway Firth shrimper, *Jean*

Loch Fyne skiff, *Snowdrop*

Portpatrick line skiff, *Brothers*

Portpatrick line skiff, *Jean Morgan*

Largs line skiff, *Laura Jane*

Other models

A further 18 models, almost all of which are the same as those mentioned above, are with family and friends, in Scotland and overseas.

GLOSSARY

BEAMS Timbers fitted across the vessel from side to side, supporting the deck.

BREASTHOOKS Strong u-shaped timbers stressing the angles between the stem and stern posts and the upper edge of the topmost strake.

BUTT The straight vertical joint of two strakes over a frame.

CARLINGS Lengths of wood running from bow to stern to support the sides of the deck or the thwarts.

CARVEL BUILT The method of boat building where the planks are joined edge to edge rather than overlapping.

CLENCH BUILT The method of building where the strakes overlap forming 'lands', and flow into each other in the last foot or so at the bow and stern. Clench building is also known as 'clinker building'.

CLEW The lower after end of a sail.

CRUTCH A vertical support towards the stern of the boat on which the lowered mainmast lies while the boat is lying to her nets.

DEADWOODS Shaped timbers sited at the acute angles between the stern, stem and keel to strengthen the keel assembly.

DIPPING LUG A sail bent on a yard where the lower forward angle of the sail is attached to a traveller, forward of the mast. To tack, the sail has to be lowered, disconnected from the traveller, swung round to the other side of the mast, secured again to the traveller and hoisted on the other tack.

FRAME A 'rib' set across the keel to which the strakes of a carvel built boat are fastened. The frame is usually constructed with three or more sections so that the grain of each section of wood lies on the long axis of the piece.

GARBOARD The strake next to the keel, fitting into the rabbet on the keel.

GUDGEONS Tube-like fittings on the stern post to receive the rod pintails fitted to the rudder.

GUNWALE The heavy timber fitted from bow to stern either outside or inside the top edge of the topmost strake. Also known as either the in-wale or the out-wale.

LANDS The overlap of the strakes of a clench-built boat where the strakes are fastened to each other.

PARREL A metal ring with wooden balls that is fitted to the mast to aid in hoisting the sail. The wooden balls prevent damage to the mast from fiction when the heavy sail is raised.

PINTAILS Fastenings on the rudder involving a set of downward facing rods that fit into the gudgeons and allow the rudder to swivel.

RABBET A groove cut into the keel and the stem and stern posts to receive the edges of the strakes.

STRINGERS Like carlings, pieces of wood fastened internally from bow to stern to support the sides of deck planks.

THWART Transverse seats in an open boat, also called 'tafts', and supported by stringers.

TRAVELLER A long U-shaped piece of metal forward of the mast to which the tack of the sail (the lower fore corner of the sail) is fastened by a hook.

TRENAILS Round pieces of wood used to fasten strakes together, whether in clench- or carvel-built boats. Trenails are lighter than metal fastenings and, as they swell when immersed in water, they are more effective in securing the strakes and other fittings.

SELECTED BIBLIOGRAPHY

Bowen, J., Ed. *Scale Model Sailing Ships*. Conway Maritime Press, 1977. ISBN 085177 111 4.

Finch, R. *Sailing Craft of the British Isles*. William Collins, 1976. ISBN 000 2197103.

Freeson, E.G. *The Construction of Model Open Boats*. Conway Maritime Press, 1975. ISBN 0 85177 080 0.

Mannering, J., Ed. *The Chatham Directory of Inshore Craft*. Chatham Publishing, 1997. ISBN 1 86176 029 9.

McCarthy, J. *Building Plank-on-Frame Ship Models*. Conway Maritime Press, 1994. ISBN 0-85177-629-9.

March E.J. *Sailing Drifters*. David & Charles (Publishers), 1978. ISBN 07153 4679 2.

——— *Sailing Trawlers*. David & Charles (Publishers), 1978. ISBN 7153 4711X

Underhill, Harold A. *Plank on Frame Models*, Volume I. Brown, Son & Ferguson, 1958/1979. ISBN 0 85174 186 X.

——— *Plank On Frame Models*, Volume II. Brown, Son & Ferguson, 1960/1981. ISBN 0 85174 292 0.

Further information

A further wealth of information and articles on ship construction can be found in the international quarterly journal, *Model Shipwright*, published by Conway Maritime Press.

Made in the USA
San Bernardino, CA
16 October 2016